Planning with Purpose

Praise for *Planning with Purpose*

"*Planning with Purpose: A Handbook for New College Teachers* is a gem. A practical guide for new college and community college instructors and graduate teaching assistants, it is a sorely needed resource, especially in fluctuating hiring processes. New English composition and literature teachers find what could be a semester long planning guide. Instructors of other subject matter courses find literacy building activities that will fit course goals of developing competent skills in literacy for their college students.

"I highly recommend this text and hope it will be widely used. It is written in a style that is readable, often entertaining, and useful for its audiences."

—Robert L. Infantino, EdD, professor of education, emeritus,
University of San Diego

"Writing exercises are only effective when they are well crafted, patiently tried out in the classroom, fine-tuned, and then tried out again. The authors of *Planning with Purpose* are expert guides to this process. Concrete explanations and useful strategies build the reader's understanding of writing for different occasions. I wish I had learned to write (assuming I ever did) through exercises like the ones contained in this book."

—José Montelongo, Maury A. Bromsen Curator of Latin American Books,
John Carter Brown Library, Providence, RI

"Even though *Planning with Purpose* is designed for newer teachers and their mentors, it has much to offer college-level teachers who have worked with students for years. In addition to thoughtful guidance on how to help students become more effective thinkers, writers, and speakers, this book offers many insights into how teachers can interact with students in productive and supportive ways. The classroom is not just a place where we engage with ideas; we also engage with one another. As I read this book, I frequently paused to think about how I can use the ideas in my own classroom. I also kept thinking to myself, 'I wish I had known that when I was a new college teacher.'

"I also have worked with hundreds, if not thousands, of college teachers across the disciplines throughout my career. As I read *Planning with Purpose*, it was readily apparent that many of the instructional practices and classroom management strategies would work effectively in general education courses in a wide range of content areas."

—Duane Roen, dean and vice provost, Arizona State University

"This book provides a resource for those who find themselves teaching college-level writing courses with minimal preparation or expertise. It acknowledges the variety of instructional and pedagogical environments in which new college instructors might find themselves, which also renders its content relevant in multiple disciplinary contexts. The text reads like a handbook, with bulleted lists broken down into questions to ask, options available, steps to take, and points of preparation to address. The authors focus on foundational concepts, such as student choice and respect for language variety, while also addressing pragmatic concerns—how to access resources, which resources to utilize and when, and how to manage grading. Their 'just in time' approach is pragmatic rather than academic, utilitarian rather than theoretical. Their objective is clear: get new college writing instructors on their feet in the classroom with greater speed, confidence, and efficacy."

—Michele Ninacs, PhD, associate professor of English, SUNY Buffalo State

Planning with Purpose

A Handbook for New College Teachers

Anna J. Small Roseboro
Claudia A. Marschall

ROWMAN & LITTLEFIELD
Lanham • Boulder • New York • London

Published by Rowman & Littlefield
An imprint of The Rowman & Littlefield Publishing Group, Inc.
4501 Forbes Boulevard, Suite 200, Lanham, Maryland 20706
www.rowman.com

6 Tinworth Street, London SE11 5AL, United Kingdom

Copyright © 2021 by Anna J. Small Roseboro and Claudia A. Marschall

All rights reserved. No part of this book may be reproduced in any form or by any electronic or mechanical means, including information storage and retrieval systems, without written permission from the publisher, except by a reviewer who may quote passages in a review.

British Library Cataloguing in Publication Information Available

Library of Congress Cataloging-in-Publication Data
Names: Roseboro, Anna J. Small, 1945- author. | Marschall, Claudia A., 1951- author.
Title: Planning with purpose: a handbook for new college teachers / Anna J. Small Roseboro, Claudia A Marschall.
Description: Lanham : Rowman & Littlefield, [2021] | Includes bibliographical references and index. | Summary: "In this book experienced educators share methods, materials, and classroom management strategies to guide and support first-year teachers"—Provided by publisher.
Identifiers: LCCN 2020042781 (print) | LCCN 2020042782 (ebook) | ISBN 9781475858204 (cloth) | ISBN 9781475858211 (paperback) | ISBN 9781475858228 (epub)
Subjects: LCSH: College teachers—Vocational guidance. | First year Teachers—Vocational guidance. | College teaching. | Classroom management.
Classification: LCC LB2331 .R62 2021 (print) | LCC LB2331 (ebook) | DDC 371.14/4—dc23
LC record available at https://lccn.loc.gov/2020042781
LC ebook record available at https://lccn.loc.gov/2020042782

To courageous scholars who accept the challenge of teaching introductory college courses while still students themselves, and to the faculty, staff, and administrators who coach, guide and mentor them.

to veteran educators in any content area who may be teaching virtually for the first time

In memory of Claudia's parents, Bernice and Frederic Marschall, who encouraged her to pursue a career in education. Their love of language, literature, and the arts has been the foundation of Claudia's studies and practice, both personally and professionally. They would be incredibly proud of her work with Anna on this book.

Contents

Acknowledgments	xi
Introduction	xiii
Note	xvi

1 Preparing to Be Effective and Efficient — 1
- Learn about Your Students — 2
- Know Where You Are Going — 3
- Schmooze the Librarians, Tech Specialists, and Teaching Cohort — 4
- Preplan Ways to Manage Grading — 9
- Conclusion — 18
- Notes — 18

2 Networking with Narratives to Cultivate Community — 19
- Explore and Write about Names — 20
- Alert: Words of Caution — 21
- Select Literary Works about Names — 22
- Read, Research, and Learn the Vocabulary of Names — 22
- Discover Interesting Cultural Information about Naming — 24
- Conclusion — 31
- Notes — 31

3 Understanding Grammars to Negotiate Conventions — 33
- Consider the Impact of Standard English with Anna's Story — 34
- Choose the Appropriate Grammar — 35
- Honor La Différence — 37

	Let Authors and Speakers Model for You	38
	Conclusion	39
	Notes	40
4	Writing to Clarify Thinking	41
	Show How Writing Is Revealing	43
	Understand Writing to Express, Explore, and Discover	43
	Clarify Teaching and Focus Study	44
	Observe Ways Student Talking Teaches	45
	Group Students in Pairs, Pods, and Small Groups	45
	Write the Steps	47
	Assign Reflective Writing: It's Valuable Even If Uncomfortable	48
	Analyze Assignment and Test Performance	49
	Conclusion	50
	Notes	50
5	Engaging Expository Writing	51
	Choose Just the Right Rhetorical Mode for the Occasion	52
	Act Out an Essay	53
	Invite Student-Choice Topics for Writing	55
	Discover Author's Purpose and Recognize Essay Patterns	56
	Set Up the Discovery Expedition	56
	Acknowledge Multiple Features in Essays	58
	Take Time for Discovery	59
	Design Extra Credit Options	60
	Teach More than Tell	60
	Conclusion	62
	Notes	62
6	Composing Compelling Arguments	63
	Build the Foundation for Convincing Argumentative Essays	64
	S.P.A.R. to Listen for Sound Arguments	65
	Take Logical Steps to Other Kinds of Writing	67
	Connect Writing to Current Events	68
	Decide How Long	69
	Use Graphics to Show Structure	70
	Write about and Exploring Visuals	70
	Enter Art and Writing about It	71
	Schedule Peer-Feedback In-Class, Then for Homework	73
	Conference to Clarify Student Thinking	74
	Prep for One-on-One Conferences	75
	Withhold Grades Until One-on-One Conferences	76

	Train for Success	77
	Release Some Control to Student Starters	77
	Most are interested in the 5Ws and H for Student Starters	77
	Conclusion	78
	Note	78
7	Writing Persuasively to Impact Thinking and Behavior	79
	Discover Ways That Compelling Arguments Precede Persuading	81
	Unveil Aristotle's Art of Rhetoric	82
	View Enhances Understanding about Fallacies	82
	Allow Students to Choose Issues That Matter	84
	Demonstrate Careful Steps to Effective Writing	85
	Use Criteria to Measure Responses to Reading and Viewing	85
	Chart Responses Provides Data for Writing	87
	Organize Notes to Write Insightful Critiques	88
	Decide and Write for a Specific Audience	89
	Write from Research: A Summative Assessment	90
	Write about an Abstract Term	90
	Review and Introduce Reference Resource Materials	91
	Use Stories and Statistics to Appeal to the Heart and the Head	93
	Connect to Current Events	94
	Organize the Researched Information	95
	Introduction	95
	Body	95
	Conclusion	95
	Allot Time to Give and Process Peer Feedback	96
	Conclusion	97
	Notes	98
8	Writing for Speaking and Multimodal Presentations	99
	Note What Makes an Effective Oral Presentation	100
	Decide the Specific Rhetorical Purpose	102
	View and Critique Public Speakers	103
	Practice by Giving a Commemorative Speech	103
	Pick a Topic and Plan the Speech	105
	Construct the Speech	105
	Incorporate Multimodal Components	107
	Organize Oral Presentations for Maximum Impact	107
	Self-Check for Effective Speaking	108
	Personalize Multimodal Presentations	109

Practice, Practice, Practice	109
Evaluate Argumentative and Persuasive Speeches	110
Conclusion	111
Notes	111
Afterword	113
Note	114
Bibliography	115
Index	117
About the Contributors	121
About the Authors	125

Acknowledgments

Teaching is both a vocation and avocation, done best in collaboration. We acknowledge first the colleagues and administrators with whom we have served. This book is a prime example of the collective wisdom gained from working with educators throughout our professional careers.

We met at an annual convention of the National Council of Teachers of English. We immediately recognized our shared passion for mentoring early career educators in pre- and post-secondary settings. After working together on multiple publications and teaching projects, we decided to combine our individual experiences and co-write this book.

Anna gives the nod to the administrators, colleagues, and professors with whom she has worked in Missouri, New York, Massachusetts, California, and Michigan. Special thanks go to Michael Teitelman who supported and entrusted her to serve in multiple leadership positions.

Claudia would like to thank Anna J. Small Roseboro for the honor and privilege of working with her. She also acknowledges the support of colleagues from the Buffalo Public Schools and Buffalo State College who provided professional and moral support and shared opportunities for professional development that have contributed to the insights described in this book.

Anna's daughter Roz Roseboro and members of her cohort of graduate teaching assistants at Northern Michigan University are the impetus for this book. They are among the recent first-year graduate teaching assistants and community college educators who contributed to this book. Their timely written reflections confirm the cultural relevance of our publication. We appreciate the input of José Luis Cano, Jr., Shanika Carter, Kelsie Endicott, Jessica Hudson, Mallory Jones, Roz Roseboro, and Tiffany Stachnik. Their full reflections will appear on the Planning with Purpose section of Anna's website www.teachingenglishlanguagearts.com and on the companion website for this book, https://planningwithpurpose.info/.

We acknowledge with gratitude the endorsers who suggested ways to include in our manuscript methods, materials, and management ideas to address the demands of educators across the content areas and those who for the first time may be teaching virtually, in hybrid settings, or fully online: Dr. Mara Lee Grayson, Dr. Robert Infantino, José Montelongo, Dr. Michele Ninacs, Dr. Duane Roen, Alison Taylor Fastov, and Dr. Nalova Westbrook.

Thanks, also, for the confidence of Tom Koerner and Carlie Wall, senior editors at Rowman and Littlefield, who expressed confidence in our work and invited us to write Planning with Purpose: A Handbook for New College Teachers. We thank Megan Delancey, who shepherded our manuscript through the production stage with such grace.

Last, but not least, we acknowledge our spouses who have been with us from the beginning: William Gerald Roseboro and Garaud MacTaggart, without whose good-natured support this project would not have been possible. Throughout the scourge of COVID 19, our husbands endured the hours of online work that have been necessary for us to complete this project on time.

Introduction

As you teach more, you will learn more.[1]

—Russell M. Nelson

Teaching students need not be the overwhelming task it poses for some new college instructors. You may be a recent college graduate, an experienced writer, or a transitioning professor assigned to teach an introductory course in your content area. You may be working with recent high school teenagers or adults older than you in a local community college or an adult school in an urban, suburban, or rural setting.

You may be a professor supervising graduate teaching assistants and first-year instructors who are assigned to content areas commonly called STEAM-O—science, technology, engineering, arts, math, or other. You may be a seasoned university educator assigned to teach online for the first time and are seeking ways to adapt what you have been doing in-person to work in a virtual setting.

This handbook is a "go-to" for graduate teaching assistants, graduate student assistants, graduate student instructors, adjuncts, fixed-term instructors, lecturers, clinical and visiting assistant professors, tenure-line professors, directors of centers for teaching and learning, deans of faculty development, and more. Community colleges, private four-year institutions, public universities, professional and vocational schools, colleges of science, engineering, and the liberal arts, will find a teaching roadmap here.

For most students, taking your course may be an eye-opening experience. They will be challenged to expand their understanding of what makes writing and speaking effective. They will wonder how critical these skills will be to their success now as students and later on the career paths of their choice. While your class may be a general education requirement for most students, it is not likely to be the only course in which they will be taught to write and speak with competence and confidence. You, therefore, do not have to stress yourself because they are not all getting top grades. Focus more on process and progress for you and for your students. As you learn to plan with purpose, teach them ways to do the same.

PLANNING WITH PURPOSE: A Handbook for New College Teachers (PWP) describes ways to

- establish a nurturing classroom environment with firm but fair grading guidelines;
- plan assignments that include strategies you can adopt or adapt; and
- balance student choice within teacher control based on course requirements.

Here are

- samples of formative and summative assessments to measure student growth in learning;
- ways to select relevant print and media texts that serve as inspiration for living and patterns for writing, and designing multimodal presentations;
- suggestions for assigning homework that extends and expands lessons you present in class and on virtual learning platforms;
- lessons designed to engage students from various cultural, ethnic, and economic populations across the nation.

Most important, here are ideas to help you manage the load by sharing the burden.

Our professional experiences serve as the bedrock on which we stand and share what we've learned. Equally important, we have invited colleagues who recently completed their first year as college teachers to share their reflections for this book. Anna is a National Writing Project Fellow. She has served as codirector and mentor of the National Council of Teachers of English Early Career Educators Leadership Award, and tutor for adult English Language Learners, trained by the Literacy Center of West Michigan. Claudia served in the Buffalo Public Schools' Mentor Teacher Internship Program, working with newly hired English Language Arts Teachers (ELA) Special Education teachers, and those with fewer than three years teaching experience, and veteran teachers transitioning to new grade levels. She also was an adjunct instructor for the Buffalo State College English Education Department's Early Field Experience course, addressing issues and concerns regarding methods, materials, and management in the classroom.

We remain current regarding issues facing educators teaching students born in the twenty-first century. Together, Anna and Claudia have served as co-chairs of the National Council of Teachers of English/English Language Arts Teacher Educators Commission to Support Early Career ELA teachers, and have co-hosted the session, "Nuts & Bolts for New ELA Teachers" at several past NCTE National Conventions.

We bring to this writing an amalgamation of our teaching and learning experiences. Equally relevant, Anna is the mother of an adult who recently completed her first year as a graduate student assigned to teach introductory composition, primarily to first-year students. Much of what Anna shared has been useful for her daughter's work and for others in that cohort. Four of them are among the seven new instructors who have contributed their reflections for this book.

College professors can find *PWP* ideas useful for preservice training sessions, and for supporting educators who are currently teaching in postsecondary classrooms across the content areas. These new graduate teaching assistants and college instructors benefit as they explore ideas related to (1) selecting texts, (2) planning engaging lessons and homework assignments, (3) managing grading, (4) varying class activities, and (5) using time efficiently with students new to the challenges in more demanding academic settings.

The progression of lessons identified above reflect the influence of Vygotsky and the National Writing Project (NWP). The first step or consideration is the gradual release of responsibility advocated by Pearson and Gallagher. Thoughtful teachers plan in-class small group and independent practice before assuming students can work independently on writing tasks. These assure the teacher that they can meet the writing and speaking outcome goals for the course. In the NWP pedagogical approach, the teacher models spiraling steps in the writing process: drafting, giving and receiving feedback, revising, and editing.

Furthermore, *PWP* describes ways teachers can include writing-to-learn and reflect on learning. From the National Writing Project's philosophical stance, all writing does *not* have to be read and/or graded by the teacher. In this book, you will see effective and efficient ways to manage the class time and assess student writing as they use it to inform, argue, persuade, entertain, and compose multimodal presentations, or just to explore, explain, and expand their thinking about literature, life, and lessons learned in your course. The pedalogical approaches: constructive, reflective, collaborative, interogative and inquiry based ideas you find in this handbook can apply to fields of study like the arts, engineering, mathematics, pre-med, social sciences, and technology for in-person and online teaching environments.

Please continue reading and learn how the methods, materials, and management strategies, and morale builders here can benefit you. They can guide and coach, support and sustain you along this first year of teaching. Explore ideas to develop and present lessons that meet students' emotional and intellectual needs while challenging them to complete increasingly

Figure 0.1   All Student Writing Need Not Be Graded. *iStock/Lamaip.*

complex tasks. What you learn can enable you to become an effective educator for whatever time you have to devote to classroom teaching. When students are learning, and you can document that learning through appropriate assessments, both you and your students enjoy more of your time together on the journey through this course of study.

NOTE

1. Russell M. Nelson, "Accomplishing the Impossible," GOODREADS (2020), accessed March 19, 2020, https://www.goodreads.com/work/quotes/47216368-accomplishing-the-impossible-what-god-does-what-we-can-do.

Chapter 1

Preparing to Be Effective and Efficient

The mediocre teacher tells.
The good teacher explains.
The superior teacher demonstrates.
The great teacher inspires.[1]

—William A. Ward

Teaching can drain one's time and energy, but intentional planning can help you use both more efficiently and effectively. Five of the most challenging tasks for educators are (1) using class time productively, (2) designing purposeful homework assignments, (3) managing grades and grading, (4) providing feedback on student work, and (5) incorporating technology that supports rather than thwarts learning, in class, partially or fully online. Like most new-to-college teachers and graduate teaching assistants (GTAs), you probably were given a set of expected course outcomes similar to those in the Writing Programs Administrators (WPA) Outcomes Statement for First-Year Composition. You are likely to see references to the rhetorical knowledge, critical thinking, reading, composing, presenting, and processing that your students should be able to demonstrate by the end of the course[2] and continue using as they pursue their postsecondary education.

This handbook, designed to mentor first-year college instructors, provides methods, materials, and management strategies for you to engage students early in your course. Descriptions for scoping out the course and implementing teacher-tested strategies will help you support their learning in practical and productive ways. So, let's get started on this journey.

It may seem odd, but a good place to begin planning and personalizing instruction is to focus on school holidays, breaks, and vacations. Aha! You recall from your own days as a student how challenging it was to be attentive the few days before and after any of these three! Among the ways you can assure your teaching stays on course is by planning assignments that maximize instruction on potentially lost days. When students understand that you know they may be distracted by other demands, they develop trust in the demands you do place on them.

LEARN ABOUT YOUR STUDENTS

While such considerations may seem difficult to effectuate on a college campus with students' attention drawn by sports, the arts, full or part-time jobs, family concerns, and social media they are worth considering. This does not mean you have to give in to their distracted behaviors, but you can plan with these possibilities in mind when in class or teaching online.

Take into consideration the ethnicities and cultures of your students. What holidays do they share in common? Which are unique to a few? How can you integrate into your lessons the wealth of information, experience, and passion surrounding holidays, breaks, and vacations? Subtler to think about is the emotional and physical drain, say, on your Jewish and Muslim students who, for cultural or religious reasons, maybe fasting on a day you planned to schedule a major assignment. Asian family lunar new year celebrations may run late into the evening. Even if your students are living on the campus, their hearts and minds may be on what their families and friends are doing at home.

In addition to knowing the cultures and ethnicities of your students, it is important to learn a little more about the circumstances in which they lived or reside now in college. How much do you know about the resources available in the community where your college is located, or where your students reside? Are there local libraries with technology available if your college does not provide it for students?

Once you have your class lists, take a look at notices regarding special physical or emotional needs. Plan time to meet with support and learning center staff with whom you will share students. Learn the requirements of your college for reporting issues that arise in the class.

What are you learning that may impact the way you set up your classroom or design lessons? Just as a tour company would gather a range of personal information before the trip begins to help ensure the safety and success of its clients, so should college teachers commit to being ready for those inherent eventualities. You want to be prepared.

Figure 1.1 What Skills Must You Teach and Assess? *iStock/Wavebreakmedia*.

KNOW WHERE YOU ARE GOING

In order to reach the outcome goals for the course you are teaching, it is essential to understand what these proficiencies—evidence of knowledge and skills—look like in practice. Planning for teaching entails figuring out how you and your students will get there from where you are now. You have used GPS, right? The first two questions usually are, "Where do you want to go?" and "Where are you now? So, this means working backwards to consider these "What?" and "How?" questions.

- What do students need to know and be able to do at the end of this course?
- How can I learn what they know and can do by then?
- What do they know already?
- How can I learn what they know and can do already?
- What kinds of lessons and experiences should I design for students
  - to show me what they know already?
  - to learn from one another?
  - to acquire the content knowledge in class or online?
  - to develop the specific skills they need to show by the end of this course? In other words,
- How will I know we have arrived at our destination?

- What resources are available—in my classroom—to my students in the classroom, on the college campus (library, dorms, learning center, in the community) or at home?
- How can I collaborate with teachers within my department and across the content areas?
- What majors, licenses, or certificates are my students pursuing?
- How can I connect what I teach to what they would like to learn?
- What will make teaching this course fun and interesting for me?
- How will I reserve time for me, with all of this work?

Once you can answer these questions—in your own words—you can begin to gather resources you have on hand. Find out what supplies are available in your department storeroom and learn the campus policy for requesting them and for printing copies. Assemble what you can to support yourselves as you work together to meet those course outcome goals.

SCHMOOZE LIBRARIANS, TECH SPECIALISTS, AND TEACHING COHORT

Librarians, media, and tech specialists can be your most precious human resources. These respected professional colleagues interact with faculty and staff across the colleges and with students from all programs across the campus. Moreover, librarians know their collections and can work with you to utilize them in ways that support lessons with culturally relevant and content specific selections. Take time to explore the library on your own, befriend the librarians and welcome the wealth of experience and knowledge they can add to your lesson planning and implementation.

There is no reason to go it alone. Tiffany Stachnik, one of our graduate teaching assistant (GTA) contributors wrote, "With a colleague, I founded the Graduate English Pedagogy Association at Northern Michigan University in an attempt to rectify teaching issues for graduate teaching assistants. In a stroke of brilliance, our organization started inviting experienced educators to our biweekly meetings to discuss pedagogy." While you may not plan something as formal as this, do not hesitate to meet regularly to share and exchange ideas with those who also are first-year college instructors. Your department leaders selected each of you for this role and you all have much to share with one another.

Making the Space Your Place

You may be sharing an office and classroom(s) with others. Still, you can personalize both places without a significant investment of money and time. For the office, it's easy to add pictures, a desk pad, and a jar of wrapped hard

Figure 1.2 Collaborating with Other Instructors Enriches Your Instruction. *iStock/monkeybusinessimages.*

candy. These can make your cubby a welcome space to hold office hours and meet with students for the one-on-one conferences many college departments require. Having candy? This just extends the hospitality tradition of sharing something to eat. Working virtually? Make a landing page with a logo or image that represent you and welcomes students.

Personalizing your classroom space may be more challenging, but with proper planning, the space can become your place. Jessica Hudson, one of our recent GTA contributors reported that she was assigned to teach in

> a former high school building on the main campus; being an older classroom, there were only two chalkboards and a small whiteboard, the latter behind the projector screen, to work with, and the static rows of heavy, unmovable desks made group activities difficult as well.

On the other hand, Kelsie Endicott, another contributor and recent first-year college teacher, taught in a variety of well-equipped rooms, but "None of the classrooms that I taught in were what I would term 'dedicated' classrooms in the sense that the space didn't belong to a particular department, so these classrooms were very nondescript."

You can make your classroom a welcoming, individualized environment just by adding visuals and music to the slides you use for class presentations. Select background colors and themes that reflect you and what you are assigned to teach. Having different colors for each unit is a good organizational strategy. The variations in color notify students that something has changed; retaining the same theme lets them know that you haven't. Create a basic set of slides to (1) welcome students, (2) list the tasks or activities for that class period, and (3) announce the coming assignments.

Then you can insert into this master file the specific lesson slides for the day. Slides can reduce excuses. Those who are speakers of other languages or who are more visual learners can look up and see. After each class, upload slides to the class website. No students who may have been absent physically or mentally should be able to say, "I didn't know."

On daily slides, insert links to detailed assignments and recommended resources to support the students as they do their homework. Links can be helpful to the students as you present your lessons in the class, and they will look familiar when students click them while doing the homework. Furthermore, you will be demonstrating what you will be asking them to do in their multimodal presentations later in the course.

Prepping Students to Use Electronic Devices and Programs

It is easy to assume students already are tech-savvy and can easily use the equipment and computer programs available on your campus. But stop a minute; recall the small snags that frustrated you when you first used a new electronic device, a new computer program, or a cell phone application.

Equally important is that the college course you are teaching likely has expectations as those described by the WPA Outcomes Statement that says, "In this Statement, 'composing' refers broadly to complex writing processes that are increasingly reliant on the use of digital technologies."[3] Check with the tech rep who can help you design lessons to show students efficient ways to navigate the technology available and give you basic ways to troubleshoot problems when—not if—they arise.

It is worth taking in-class or online time to review the use of devices each time you begin a new course. If you know they know how to navigate the systems, it will not be difficult to hold students accountable for utilizing them both for in-class and homework assignments. Because some students will be new to your college or others may be unfamiliar with the programs you plan to use, prepare for an in-class demonstration during the second class meeting with

- a protocol for using devices in your classroom (i.e., turn off phone ringers, turn tablets over when you are speaking and expecting them to be watching

you or viewing slides, mute microphones in virtual sessions, and other basic behaviors to enhance their learning when they are with you).
- a class list with student school-assigned login names and general password to your college learning platform. (Blackboard, Canvas, EduCat, Moodle, or other.)
- a tally to see which students know how to use which word processing program best: Word, Google Docs, Adobe Acrobat, other? Avoid frustration by learning who knows what now.
- Information on logging in using their school ID. For some students, this will be a no-brainer; for others, a brain strain. Take time now; avoid confusion later.
- how to create a password. (Some colleges have specific requirements for passwords.)
- how to navigate the specific program(s) you have chosen for doing their first assignment.
- slides to demonstrate key steps for each of these tasks. (Save for later reviews.)
- a short video tutorial that reviews the steps for using the program or learning platform.
- screenshots showing what students should see on their devices when they get to specific steps in the program and enter the website you set up for the course.
- a short assignment to complete during the class meeting. This could be sending you an email using the school learning platform with "HELLO from (their last name)" in the subject line. In the body of the email, include three things the student hopes to learn in this class, based on the syllabus you discussed already.
- a timer to ring 7 minutes before the class ends to allow time for students to shut down their devices and give you their attention for closing announcements.

Circulate and assist as needed. Invite students familiar with the technology to be teaching assistants for the day. By preparing and accepting help, you can reduce the frustration of getting students online, into the school portal, and having a successful experience when they are away from the class and doing homework. Consider using Zoom rooms for student groups or pairs to practice and share insight about using learning platform your college uses.

Avoid mutual exasperation. Note what Roz Roseboro, one of our GTA contributors, wrote in her reflection about the first time she scheduled an in-class peer response activity:

> My intentions were sound—my execution was not. I learned that I shouldn't ever assume anything and anticipate where a process could break down. Next

time around, I'll be much more explicit in my instruction and limit some choices that could introduce unwanted and potentially troublesome variability ... Students will not always do what they're told. Students will lie. I shouldn't assume ANYTHING. Lesson learned.

If your class meets just once a week, resist giving homework that requires the use of technology until after the second class meeting. First, go by the old fashioned route and provide handouts in emails. Why have students expend valuable time trying to figure out navigation on those devices that could be better spent reading and/or writing in preparation for the next class meeting? Why should you be equally frustrated? New students may fail to upload assigned work, just because they have not yet figured out how to use electronic resources. Rest assured. Both your tech newbies and those who are tech-savvy will appreciate your thoughtfulness. You will be using valuable class time to ensure that more can stay on target to learn what is assigned for that course—and inviting them to pair up while learning and practicing navigation gets them started toward that course outcome goal of collaborative learning.

Assigning Purposeful Homework

A good rule of thumb is to design homework assignments that can be completed in the same number of hours students spend in the class. Then, decide why that homework assignment is being given; what purpose it serves: to (1) practice, (2) prepare, (3) polish, or (4) ponder what they are learning. Is the assignment to practice something taught in the class? Is the assignment to gather and organize information, to read or write and prepare for the next class meeting? Metacognition is useful, too. If so, in the next class, use what students have prepared. Otherwise, they are less likely to do what feels like busywork.

Is the homework assignment to polish a section of a paper, product (posters, slide shows, videos), or oral presentation? Direct student attention to the instructions and rubric for that assignment. Is the goal of the homework to polish a presentation to assure students can advance their slides, access their video, manage the props, use their notes smoothly within the time requirements? Is homework to write self-reflection? Consider giving full credit for the homework completed on time. Keep records, read so you'll know how they are doing, but don't grade. Most importantly, use what you assign.

Guiding Principles for Behavior and Decorum

College students can be marvelous and mischievous. Think about ways to maximize the former and minimize the latter. Reflect on what you can and can't stand in terms of classroom behavior, absences and tardies, homework deadlines, movement and noise in the classroom, and flexibility for assignments. Prepare notes on how you will outline acceptable classroom behavior for your students.

Experienced educators often have three or four general principles that can be applied in specific situations. Consider, as a start, those that refer to attendance, homework, and student behavior: (1) be present, (2) be prepared, and (3) participate courteously.

Once you decide your three or four guiding principles, include them on your class handouts, your website, on major assignments, and on your official syllabus at the beginning of the course. It is essential for all to know the basic principles by which you plan to conduct your class. It also is good for students to be reminded throughout the course.

When they understand the reasons for rules, students usually respond with compliance rather than scathing sarcasm. Some colleges have campus-wide behavior statements and attendance policies that you are expected to follow with little or no tweaking.

PREPLAN WAYS TO MANAGE GRADING

Your students may question what you do just because it is so different from what they have experienced. Note here, ways to (1) manage grading with customized rubrics, (2) utilize general grading guidelines, (3) handle late work, and (4) offer extra credit options. If you understand and can articulate the progress of skills and knowledge acquisition you are required to report, you can plan more efficiently, and students understand early what and how they must show what they know. See online gradebook in learning platform.

Customizing Rubrics

Now that you have a better understanding of what students are expected to know and be able to do in terms of composing and presenting by the end of the course, develop or adapt a general rubric. A rubric is a standard document that describes specific traits one expects to see in papers, products (posters, slide shows, videos), and oral presentations.

If your department does not have such a document, consider adapting the Six Traits rubric published by Education Northwest. It has descriptive statements on CONTENT IDEAS, ORGANIZATION, VOICE, WORD CHOICE, SENTENCE FLUENCY, and CONVENTIONS; recent forms have added PRESENTATION. Share the general rubric with your students early, but not on the first class meeting. The students will be overwhelmed with information. Then, customize this rubric for subsequent assignments. For example, to specify what is required in terms of

- CONTENT, when students are writing about a specific text, customize the rubric stating that they include references and/or quotations from the beginning, middle, and end of the assigned or chosen reading.
- For research, customize CONTENT for that assignment and add that for minimum credit, students must include evidence from three to five different kinds of sources.
- For WORD CHOICE and SENTENCE FLUENCY, specify on the rubric to use academic terms correctly, specific jargon selected for the chosen audience, and weave quotations and transition words seamlessly into their own writing.
- In terms of CONVENTIONS, after reviewing/teaching students how to cite sources, add words like "includes a bibliography and punctuates quotations correctly."

For inexperienced writers, you may find that page numbers in parentheses after quotations or direct references, and an alphabetized list of sources consulted will suffice early in the course. By the end of the course, however, all students should be required to use endnotes and construct bibliographies in the specific style used at your college or in your specific content area.

Begin using the rubric on the first major assignment. However, before you review or teach a specific skill, there is no need to mark students down significantly for not exhibiting that feature. But, once a trait is reviewed, modeled, and practiced, customize your rubric, reminding students that grades now will reflect their skill at exhibiting that trait and using that convention correctly. In science, technology, engineering, arts, math and other content area classes, see the specific style and organization patterns for your department.

Grading Guidelines

Just as you like knowing what is expected of you, the same is true for students. On a road trip, you look for signs indicating how close you are to your destination. When you see familiar topography or promised landmarks, you relax a bit and breathe a little easier. The same can be true about grading as it relates to you and your students. Students should not be surprised by the grades they earn. Some students, because of other commitments, may settle for a B rather than put in the time to earn the A. That's okay. It's their choice.

Fewer students challenge their grades when they have had clearly written instructions to which they can refer before submitting their work. For that reason, offer a set of general grading principles that can be applied to most assignments. Explain these guidelines early in the course, but not on the first class meeting. Students will already be overwhelmed with the newness of everything! You can, however, have something like the following posted on your website and on any general handouts you distribute on opening day, or include in emails you send to welcome students to your course.

C = Complete (includes all components of the assignment).
B = Complete and Correct (minimal errors in mechanics, usage, grammar and spelling, citations).
A = Complete, Correct, and Creative (original, fresh, something special that enhances final paper, performance, or product—posters, slide shows, videos).
D = Deficient (Missing required components listed on the assignment sheet).
F = Failed to submit the assignment for assessment in a timely fashion.

Customize your rubrics with the traits on which the written paper, video, slideshow, or oral presentation will be graded. Provide a specific rubric for

Figure 1.3 Share Grading Guidelines with Students and Administrators. *iStock/Liubov Trapeznykova.*

those graded assignments weighted heavily enough to have a major impact on course grades. Rubrics and grading guidelines provide the same comfort as a map or the voice on a GPS when traveling in an unfamiliar territory. They help plan your trips and guide you along the way.

Winning with Late Work Coupon and Extra Credit Options

Some experienced educators build in flexibility from day one, and you can, too. For example, at the beginning of the course, provide each student with a one-time use coupon worth 5 percent of the assignment points (or the difference between a B and a B+). When turning in the assignment late will not negatively impact the work of your other students, there is little reason not to accept late work turned in within a week of the due date. This late coupon can be used to avoid incurring whatever late penalty you will have set in your course. It's a fact that few instructors can grade all the assignments on a single night anyway. And, if a student spends another couple of days polishing the paper or product, it will take less time to grade.

This late option usually is not offered for oral in-class presentations. Being a week late could seriously throw off the schedule for the whole class. Instead, allow students to have their choice of scheduled presentation days. They know their out-of-class commitments and can avoid conflicts as much as possible. It also is fine to allow students, with your permission, to switch presentation dates with a consenting classmate. Be flexible when it doesn't negatively impact class progress or your grading time.

What is attractive about this coupon offer is that the point value for a student's unused late-pass coupon can be added to overall points before you compute final grades. Most students who have had an off-day and earned fewer points on an earlier assignment will be glad to "cash in" this coupon at the end of the course. Set up a column in your online grade book to account for this coupon. Note: change that number to a negative to indicate points have been used.

Another flexibility option is to build in ways students can earn extra credit without creating extra work for yourself. Watch for examples in the chapters to come for ways students can earn 10 or 15 extra points being a student starter, as described in chapter 6, or completing a short, focused critique on the presentation by a campus or community guest speaker as described in chapter 8. Consider tasks that allow students to utilize skills you are teaching, but don't overload you with grading. Have a maximum number of points earnable as extra credit.

Late and extra credit work should be turned in by the week BEFORE the final week of the class. You do not need to be swamped at this time in the course. However, if extenuating circumstances arise, take them into consideration. But don't be a pushover. You have work to complete in a timely fashion. Building in flexibility can be a win, win, win situation. You will be firm, fair, and flexible, three characteristics students appreciate in their teachers, instructors, and professors.

Increasing Weight on Assignments

At the start of the term, big assignments need not be weighted heavily enough to "kill" a grade for the course. Keep the standards high for processed papers, projects, and presentations on which students have time to plan, get peer feedback, and revise. Then increase the weight as the course unfolds. Students who have time to learn the standards and get feedback on their performance are seldom so discouraged that they stop trying.

You may plan 1,500 points for the course. Daily work completed on time earns full credit. Peer feedback done in the class or by students as homework can be worth 10–50 points. Both daily writing and providing feedback serve as practice for students and formative assessments—insight measuring progress by both the students and you.

For example: Subdivide the assignments with points for each step in the process of completing the paper, product, or presentation: 10 percent for prewrite/proposal; 30 percent for draft; 15 percent for providing feedback; 40 percent for final draft, and 5 percent for self-reflection with student including their anticipated grade based on the rubric designed for that assignment. For example,

- 200 Points for a NARRATIVE assignment.
- 300 Points for EXPOSITORY/INFORMATIVE assignment.
- 400 Points for PERSUASIVE/ARGUMENTATIVE assignment.
- 500 Points for MULTIMODAL PRESENTATION w/written, visual, and oral components.
- 100 Points for Optional assignments.

Designing Lessons with Common Components

Preplanning and pacing are equally important to maximizing the class time for efficient and effective instruction. You will find your lesson delivery flowing more smoothly if you adapt the "I, We, They" approach. Consider these questions as you plan and scaffold your lesson, offering small steps to success:

- "What can *I* present and model during this class meeting?"
- "What can *we* do together to practice, discuss, and reflect on what I present and model?"

- "What can *they*, the students, do to implement independently what they've just experienced in my presentation, during their interaction with partners, in small groups, or in the whole-class discussion?"

Even veteran classroom teachers use timers to help them stay on task. Try it to see how it works for you. You could plan 5–7 minutes for class starters. If you are teaching a composition class, it is valuable to have your students writing something every day. Many educators trained in the writing process theory of the National Writing Project (NWP) have students keep journals in which they write something at the start of each class period. Educators who teach math, science, and engineering may assign warm-up problems for students to practice recently learned skills. Language instructors may dictate short passages for students to transcribe as a way to practice listening and writing skills.

Journal writings are ungraded exercises, so assigning them need not be a grading burden for you. Your task will be to decide what topic or kind of writing will be helpful as you teach them how to write narratives, an expository or informative essay, argumentative or persuasive essays that they may also adapt for oral presentations. Often these writings and warm-up activities spark conversations that stimulate learning.

Question? Oh, what kind of prompts should you consider? Anything about which students can write in 5–7 minutes with the option of sharing or not sharing with a partner or small group. Multiple websites include lists of prompts. Search with these words, "journal writing prompts," and then select those you believe will engage your students. One popular site posts 180 Writing Prompts! Similar sites have STEM and STEAM-O warmups

Do not hesitate to choose seemingly simple prompts or tasks. Warmups do not have to be hard to be good. The goal is to have students exercise their minds: selecting words, and constructing sentences, reflecting on what they have seen and heard, read, and experienced. All may be utilized in the writing, thinking, and work they must do for your class.

On some days, you may give them a prompt based on a reading you provide that day or one they had been assigned to read as homework. In either case, have copies of that reading in the class or linked online. Whatever you choose should focus student attention on a new topic for the day or reflect on homework assignments given recently.

If students must read, view a diagram, picture, or quick video clip before writing, allot more time for this activity. Then plan the next 15–20 minutes for a mini-lesson during which you describe an upcoming assignment, review lessons already taught, or relay what you observed on their homework or last graded assignment. Regularly teach in different modalities. Show short video clip, project, or distribute copies of a writing text you reference as an example of a reading, writing, or speaking strategy. Such visuals are readily available online.

Borrowing to Support Lesson Presentation

Creating teaching slides need not be all that tough to do. The topics in introductory courses across the content areas are similar to those taught on campuses across the country, so plan to borrow resources to support those lesson presentations. Just do a web search for the topic of the day. Find a set of slides that are close to your goals, download, and modify the slides to fit your needs.

Consider incorporating short video clips to illustrate what you're teaching or simply to have another voice reiterating key ideas you want to drive home. Much of the work is already done. However, you are responsible for what is taught in your class, so be sure to check carefully the contents of any set of slides and adapt them to support the philosophy of your department and the specifics of your presentation for the day. Remember to cite sources on the closing screen of the slide file.

As you prepare teaching slides, consider setting the first eight or ten slides to advance automatically for about 5 minutes. These could be the slides with the welcome image or quotation, the topic for the day, the opening writing prompt or warm-up task, a thought for the day, and where you'd like students to be seated for the day or grouped in virtual meeting rooms.

It's a good practice to rearrange the seating periodically to give students opportunities to work in different configurations, in person, or in ZOOM or GOOGLE breakout rooms. Listing the activities planned for the day signals the students what to expect and reminds you to deliver what you planned. You can make one set of opening slides, then copy and paste those four or five times so that the slides advance but repeat. Students soon arrive in anticipation, view, get settled, and are ready to get to work right away once the class period begins. The set of slides you post to the website after the class need not have the repetitions but don't worry about taking them out if you don't have time. Repetition is better than no slides posted.

Encouraging Contemplative Student Talk

To bring the students into the learning experience, it is important to pause and give them time to process what you have presented. You could project a slide with two or three questions inviting students to choose one and write a quick summary of what you've just presented. Then, for 5–7 minutes, have them TURN AND TALK with a partner or a small group about what they have written. This is a version of the THINK, PAIR, SHARE strategy that can be implemented one or more times in a single class meeting. Circulate around the room as students talk. Observe, listen, and conduct a formative assessment during which you discover what seems to be clear and what may need further explanation. In virtual settings, drop into virtual breakout rooms.

You could then ask students to read aloud their summaries. It's okay to have repetition. Or, if you are pressed for time, ask, "Who has something to add to that summary?" until everyone has had an opportunity to speak. Then, have a way for students to practice what you've just taught or demonstrated. They usually appreciate being able to work on segments of upcoming assignments.

Include multimedia components in weekly activities. Invite students to bring them. They are an authentic way for students to practice what you are teaching, to learn with and from one another, and an informal way for you to measure what they are learning.

Neutralizing Excuses

Include links in the HOMEWORK slide you upload on the class website. Simply state the instructions for what they are expected to do, include a couple of links to sample websites on the topic, mention how the homework will be counted (100% for completion on time), and where and in what format the homework is to be uploaded on the class website.

It may take a month or so before students are consistent about checking there regularly; this practice will be new to many of them. Still, do not give them outs or excuses when you are giving them a zero for not following the directions. Upload the slides for written homework guidelines. Don't rely on verbal or long-term printed instructions.

Maximizing Movement to Motivate Learning

Plan and incorporate a variety of in-class activities that get your students up and moving, turning, and talking about the topic of the day in your particular course. You may project simple prompts for THINK, PAIR, SHARE responses as a middle-of-the-class challenge. Build in breaks during virtual teaching sessions so students can get up and walk around. Have students working together in small groups to analyze a text, to locate samples of composition or content theory applications, to prewrite together as peers, or plan for the next assignment. Remember, one of the WPA outcome goals is collaborative learning. If you do all the work, you do all the learning.

Many GTAs find that games are great generators of interest and engagement. The challenge will be to find games that expand and explore what you're tasked to teach. You may create the game yourself or invite students to locate them online to share with the class. Some teachers use prepared and adaptable games like KAHOOTS and JEOPARDY, which draw on knowledge of topics in multiple content areas. It's important to incorporate a variety of speaking and listening, viewing, and writing activities for each class meeting. Movement motivates. So, plan purposefully.

Add music to the slides to create the mood for the day. You may choose the same music, calm but not soporific, that is inviting and tone-setting as the theme that plays most days. On different days, when you're doing something special, use different music. This will alert students to be attentive to discover what's going on. Your space will be a place to which students arrive with expectations and curiosity. Both are attitudes that enhance learning.

Yes, this personalization takes time, but it is part of effective planning. As you create the slides, you are reflecting, focusing, and refining what you are to teach that meeting. As you choose the opening prompt or task, you are considering what you want the students to know and be able to do that day.

When they know what to expect when they arrive, students tend to come ready to do what is planned. When you know they will be ready to go, you don't have to use valuable time motivating them to get going! And, you can take attendance as they get settled, watching the slides, and listening to music. Attendance, in some colleges, is figured into course grades, and can be tallied in most online course management programs. Be sure you understand the policy at your college and keep good records.

Pacing Class Time

To make time run smoothly, it is important to arrive at your room early enough to have your technology set up and ready to go. If you have brought handouts, have them clipped in bundles so you can quickly disperse one bundle per table or row, therefore, getting that task done expeditiously. In a virtual setting, have the applications open on your desktop so you can share screens quickly.

Once the official class time begins, students are settled, and attendance is recorded, you can briefly use slides to give an overview of your I-We-They plan for the day. You could (1) begin with your 15–17-minute mini-lesson presentation; (2) follow with a 10–15-minute interactive component for students to process what you've presented; then (3) allot 10–15 minutes for individuals to practice independently; and finally, (4) close with 5 minutes of reflecting on the class time together in an oral summary and a written exit slip. If your class meets for more than an hour, give them a break after this first cycle, repeat it, expanding and extending the topic for the day.

Including a timer on the slides helps pace yourself. When the timer chimes or buzzes, allow students to complete the sentence they're working on, then don't close, but pull down the laptop screen or turn over their tablets and give you their attention. Establishing a dependable routine helps both students and teachers use time more efficiently.

Arriving early and getting set up, meeting, and greeting students as they enter the classroom sets the tone for the class meeting. Having a buzzer set to ring 5 minutes before the class ends helps you close in an orderly fashion, free to stand at the door, collect exit slips, and say goodbye as the students leave the space that you have made your place during that class meeting.

CONCLUSION

Ways to schedule and implement in-class and online peer feedback are described in greater detail in the upcoming chapters on writing to clarify thinking, to inform, to persuade, and to give multimodal oral presentations. Whether you are a physicist or statistician, or a Germanophile, group work is central to student learning. For now, move on to discover ways to create a collaborative community of learners. Begin the journey with students and instructor getting to know and trust one another enough to write freely and give courteous and constructive feedback. Applying these skills across the content areas enhances the experience for all. Travel along learning with and from each other as each of you develop as a writer, speaker, consumer, and producer of media. Yes, teaching is another way of learning.

NOTES

1. William Arthur Ward, *Brainy Quotes*, accessed March 6, 2020, https://www.brainyquote.com/authors/william-arthur-ward-quotes.
2. Council of Writing Program Administrators, 2020, "WPA Outcomes Statement for First-Year Composition (3.0)," Last Modified, July 18, 2019, http://wpacouncil.org/aws/CWPA/pt/sd/news_article/243055/_PARENT/layout_details/false.
3. Ibid.

Chapter 2

Networking with Narratives to Cultivate Community

Getting to know you,
getting to know all about you.
Getting to like you,
getting to hope you like me.[1]

—Oscar Hammerstein

Even in the age of electronic social networking, in-person relationships are the most meaningful for teachers and learners. The classroom itself is a "site" for social networking among increasingly diverse students, first-year classroom instructors, and graduate teaching and student assistants (GTA/GSIs). To prepare for learning on this journey, it is essential to prime the pump, increase the flow of ideas, and ready students to work together to explore, explain, and express themselves in multiple oral and written formats. The Council of Writing Program Administrators (WPA) says in its course outcome goals that by the end of the first-year, college students should be able

- *To participate effectively in collaborative processes . . .*
- *To review work-in-progress for the purpose of developing ideas before surface-level editing*[2]

Telling stories and writing narratives are effective and efficient ways to begin meeting these course goals.

You may have planned a couple of ice-breaker activities for the first day to help your students get to know one another and you. Now, how about considering a narrative writing assignment based on names to discover your students' current writing agility and to assess how nimble they are at conducting research? This sample lesson includes options that informally assess skills your students bring to class, whether basic composition, introductory science, math, or social studies.

EXPLORE AND WRITE ABOUT NAMES

We must wear our names within all the noise and confusion of the environment in which we find ourselves; make them the center of all our associations with the world, with man and with nature. We must charge them with all our emotions, our hopes, hates, loves, aspirations. They must become our masks and our shields, and the containers of all those values and traditions which we learn and/or imagine as being the meaning of our familial past.[3]

—Ralph Ellison, "Hidden Name and Complex Fate"

Names are important. They can distinguish one thing from another and link a person to families, cultures, and communities. Names can make students proud or embarrassed, one with others, and separate from others. This paradox of emotions poses a challenge and an opportunity. This enigma makes for an intriguing way to communicate culture and identity with lessons that can help establish a community of supportive learners who know about

Figure 2.1   Get to Know Them. Write Away. *iStock/Prostock-Studio.*

one another and become willing to share their writing and exchange feedback with classmates.

Depending on your college or university, students in your class may be away from home for the first time or attending college where they know no one else. Many are freshmen, eager to become independent of their parents or guardians, often straining against the ties that bind them. These young adults are developing their self-identities distinct from that of their families. Among your students, maybe those taking their first college classes as grown-ups, considerably older than their classmates. Writing about names can build a trusting learning community in a nonthreatening way. Perhaps it is because the students will be doing what so many like to do best—talking about themselves!

ALERT: WORDS OF CAUTION

Writing about names, however, may evoke trigger moments, causing emotional difficulties for some students. So be sensitive to the fact that some may resist this project for personally traumatic reasons. Be prepared to adapt rather than scrap this getting-to-know-you assignment.

Consider the ethnicities of your students. Discussing the issue of names and ancestry proves to be difficult for some students and impossible for others. Prior to the 1860s, the birth records of African Americans included few surnames and, when kept at all, first names often were recorded among the cattle records. Even in the twenty-first century, few African Americans can trace their ancestry more than a few generations. Those families who can trace their history may already know that they carry the surnames of slave owners. Most know that their families originated on the continent of Africa, but few have access to information that can verify the country or the tribe.

Families of new-to-America students may have come to escape political unrest in their country of origin. Some students may be able but unwilling to discuss their names. Ancestors may have changed their names as protection against political repercussions. On the other hand, such students may appreciate the fact that you are interested in learning more about their culture and are thrilled with the opportunity to talk about it.

A teacher new to the campus or community knows to confer with veteran educators at the college and then adapt the lessons as needed to gain the benefits and avoid the pitfalls. The more diverse your school's community, the more careful you need to be. Consider adapting the assignment so the writings can be based on real or imagined incidents. Remember, the goal is to assess current writing abilities.

With so many pitfalls, why bother? Because just reading texts about naming and living with names can be a rich, intellectual experience for your students!

In addition, the accompanying assignments help meet several course outcome goals in interesting and illuminating ways as you design lessons for

- reading, discussing, and analyzing texts in a variety of genres.
- learning content-specific vocabulary.
- conducting various kinds of research (online, library, and interview).
- writing brief autobiographical sketches for a narrative assignment.
- participating in peer editing groups.
- giving oral reports.

SELECT LITERARY WORKS ABOUT NAMES

One way to begin is with a lesson you can simply call "What's in a Name?" based on Sandra Cisneros' "My Name," a chapter from *The House on Mango Street*. This is her autobiographical vignette about growing up as a child of Mexican immigrants in Chicago. Follow up with "Hidden Name and Complex Fate," an essay by Ralph Ellison, an African American named by his father for Ralph Waldo Emerson, the renowned American poet. The Ellison essay works incredibly well as a springboard for writing stories based on experiences living with one's names.

Read "Hidden Name/Complex Fate" to see how students handle nonfiction essay texts. Point out that expository writing uses text structures they may have learned in high school. Students may even recall the terms: description, sequence, cause and effect, compare and contrast, and problem and solution. If necessary, find and show an online video as a mini-lesson to review these structures with your students. Ellison's essay inspired the questions you can use for the students' research and writing about their own names. (See table 2.1.)

Begin both readings during the class. Doing so gives you an opportunity to informally assess students' approaches to different genres. This knowledge will help you design future lessons based on the skill levels of the students in your class. One of the WPA outcome goals relates to reading analytically and critically. Start now to determine what skills your students have and which you may need to design lessons to help them learn.

READ, RESEARCH, AND LEARN
THE VOCABULARY OF NAMES

As an educator, you know the value of reading and analyzing model texts to discover their effectiveness. Paying attention to organizational patterns,

Table 2.1 Research Your Names

1. Use a dictionary and/or online resources to find out what each of your own names means.
2. Interview a family member to learn the sources of your name(s). If you have equipment, audiotape or videotape the interview. Who named you and why? Are you named for a friend or family member? Someone else?
3. Determine the kind of surname or last name you have. Is it a place name, like Al-Fassi, Hall, or Rivera; an occupation, like Chandler, Smith, or Taylor; a descriptive, Braun or Strong; or a patronymic or version of a father's name, like Ben-Yehuda, McNeil, or Von Wilhelm?
4. Describe incidents you have experienced because of your name, including mispronunciations, misspellings, and misunderstandings.
5. Write about nicknames and related embarrassing or humorous experiences.
6. Identify challenges you feel because of the name(s) you carry.

diction, and sentence structure helps readers focus on reasons the writing works for the purpose intended. For this assignment, you may want to introduce content-specific vocabulary of naming: surname, given name, nickname, nom de plume, pseudonym, pen name, and alias.

Encourage students to interview a family member to gather information about how and why the students have come to have the names they carry. You may need to review with your student researchers the correct way to cite an interview in the text of the essay and to format their bibliographies based on the style used at your college.

With expanded resources available on the Internet, most students are able to find enough information to fulfill the basic purposes of the assignment—to consider their own names, conduct research, and write about family or cultural traditions of naming that they discover. If students have uncommon names or common names that are spelled uncommonly, they may need a bit of help identifying similar, researchable alternatives. Prepare them by showing them different spellings of the same name, such as Anna, Ana, Ann, Anne, Annie, Anouska, Anya, and even Hannah.

Students might benefit from using ancestry.com and similar websites to collect historical information about their family names. By all means, share your name story and write along with your students.

As students consider responses to these prompts, they reflect on who they are in their families, the college, the wider community, and perhaps even the world. Some students may learn family history never previously discussed. Others awaken tender memories of relatives and family friends for whom they have been named. Some may be sadly embarrassed, others pleasantly surprised.

DISCOVER INTERESTING CULTURAL INFORMATION ABOUT NAMING

This research assignment is a good one to introduce students to one of several ways to give and receive courteous and constructive feedback. As students read about name-related experiences during peer-response sessions, they discover surprising naming traditions observed in the families of their classmates. They might learn that in some villages in India, all the girls in a family may have the same middle name; or that some Thai families carry extremely long, polysyllabic names, like Prachyaratanawooti, for which each syllable represents a generation the family has lived in that region. Students might learn that in some families, it is the grandmother who chooses grandchildren's names, that the eldest son always is named for his father, or that the middle name for all the children is their mother's maiden name.

Your students may notice interesting combinations of Anglo and Asian or Spanish names. Some students find out that their families' names have been Americanized to avoid discrimination based on ethnicity, religion, or nationality. A number of your students may have saints' day names or hyphenated last names that include both their mother's maiden name and their father's last name. Some learn the spelling of their surnames is simply the result of an error made when their ancestors entered the country through Ellis Island in New York or Angel Island in San Francisco. No one ever bothered to correct the mistake.

One of the assignment prompts invites students to talk about the challenges of living with their names, as described in the essay by Ralph Ellison, "Hidden Name and Complex Fate." Some student writing may reveal that carrying the name of a particularly famous or infamous relative causes them discomfort. One young man named for his father, a prominent businessman in the community, may acknowledge in his essay that he felt unworthy to be called Robert and insisted that his peers call him Robbie, a diminutive version of the father's strong name. Cecilia, a talented singer, was depressed for a few days on learning that the name she loves means "blind one" then jubilant after discovering that St. Cecilia is the patron saint of music and musicians.

Other students may write about the embarrassment of having to correct the pronunciation of their names at the beginning of every school year and the frustration of having to spell their names everywhere they go. These reminders of sensitivity surrounding names remind us to learn to pronounce and spell each student's name as early in the course as possible. It is just another way of honoring each one as an individual with his or her own special names.

Springboarding to Writing Narratives about Names

Distribute a copy of the vignette "My Name" by Sandra Cisneros, and prepare to conduct a "jump-in reading" activity to help students get a feel for the style and to think about what the writer may be saying to them. First, ask students to read silently, underlining words or phrases that catch their attention. Then you read the vignette out loud, asking students again to underline words or phrases they think are interesting or important.

Finally, starting at the beginning again, invite one student to begin reading, stopping at the first mark of punctuation. Others jump in to read without being called upon and read to the next punctuation mark. If more than one student begins reading at the same time, urge each to listen to the other(s) and to read as one voice. Between voices, let the silence resonate.

Students may be uncomfortable at first, giggle a bit, but soon catch on. The silence between the sounds of different single voices and combinations of multiple voices leaves indelible impressions and elicits powerful results in the next step of this assignment—writing.

To help the students get started composing their narratives, after reading "My Name," ask them to do a "quick write." A quick write is short, nonstop writing on an assigned topic. For a brief spurt of time—3 to 5 minutes—students let their thoughts flow without censoring them. In this assignment, ask students to copy an underlined phrase or sentence from the reading. Then use that phrase or sentence as a jumping-off point to write rapidly about their own names. Write along with them. The following is a quick write based on Cisneros's piece:

"My Name" A Quick Write Inspired by
Sandra Cisneros's Vignette of the Same Name

Anna Jamar Small Roseboro. Is this *"me"*? My name is a combination of my paternal grandmother's, Anna; my maternal grandmother's, Jamie; my dad's name, Small; and my husband's name, Roseboro. Everyone has had my name—made something of it, then passed it along to me. Anna means *"gift of God."* Is it I who am the gift or my grandmother who is a gift to me? Jamie is short for Jamar. My grandmother, whose full name is Jamar Elna, is named for her four aunts, Jane, Martha, Ellen and Nora—what a burden, what a privilege, to carry the names of so many relatives. Or is it a blessing? Am I standing on the shoulders of those who've come before me?

Small, my maiden name always caused me trouble. *"Small,"* they'd tease. *"You're not small; you're tall!"* I was always the tallest girl in my elementary school classes. In high school, however, I used the name to my advantage. I ran for a senior class office. My slogan was, *"Good things come in Small packages."* Finally, success with that name.

Then, I married Bill Roseboro during the years that Johnny Roseboro was a star catcher for the L.A. Dodgers. He'd been in the news because of a fight with

Juan Marichal. Everywhere I went, *"Are you related to Johnny Roseboro?"* *"Yes, but what has that to do with me?"* Who am I really?

Extending the Experience or Keeping It Brief

Yes, it is worth allotting class time for an assignment like this because it is a useful way to do four things important to success in any course. It's an efficient way to

- get to know the students.
- introduce or review basic writing process concepts: prewriting, drafting, giving and receiving feedback before revising.
- discover students' prior knowledge, academic vocabulary, and writing strategies they already know.
- provide an opening assignment most will find interesting to complete.

One professor made this "Living With a Name," an interview assignment during which students, working in pairs, interviewed one another. They next wrote about what they learned, then introduced their partner to the class, using what they learned in the interview. Assignments that start with students talking and writing about themselves in ways that are comfortable to them and informative to their classmates help create a community of learners.

If you decide to extend this unit beyond the first few class meetings, consider substituting or reading a chapter from Richard Kim's *Lost Names*, about Korean families forced by the government of Japan to adopt Japanese names; *Not Even My Name*, an autobiographical work by Thea Halo about Pontic Greeks in Turkey; or *The Namesake*, a novel by Jhumpa Lahiri, about the naming traditions of a family from India.

Let your own interest, the cultures, and interests of your students guide your selections each time. As always, select readings to fit your current setting, texts that serve as windows for seeing others, and mirrors for seeing oneself. Consider inviting students to write about the names of key figures in your content areas like Einstein for science and math; James Lipton in the arts; Alan Turing in technology; Dolores Huerta or John Lewis for history. To keep this personal, encourage students to research and write about someone with a name that begins with the same letter as the student's first or last name.

Giving and Receiving Peer Feedback

Most first-year composition course outcome goals include having students know when, why, and how to give and receive courteous constructive feedback. Having instructors who are also the guide from the side can be more valuable than their being only the sage from the stage. In other words, design lessons for which students learn to do more for one another instead of depending only on you.

In this book are several ways to organize the class sessions during which students give and receive peer feedback that lead to meaningful revision. The challenge, however, may be motivating students to revise. Jessica Hudson, one of our GTA contributors, highlights "issue with teaching revision: lack of motivation. For many students, it seems once it's written, it's written. They're not interested in seeing how it could be improved because they don't see the worth in it already!" Motivation seldom is a problem when students are writing about themselves. As you foster a safe community of writers, students learn how to communicate in supportive ways that challenge themselves and their peers to improve their composition and communication skills.

Starting with a R.A.G.

A read-around group (R.A.G.) session for giving and receiving peer feedback works well at the start of most courses. Students bring to the class a printed draft of their name essay. You provide a simple version of your grading rubric. (See sample in chapter 1.) Arrange circles of five or six students. Once settled, you review with them the rubric with traits on which the final narrative essay will be evaluated. This rubric, a chart with numbers (1–5), to rate the traits will guide students' reading and commenting about the drafts of their peers.

While most students will have devices on which to work electronically, consider doing this first R.A.G. activity with pens and paper. Once students are comfortable with the process, they can transfer that knowledge when working on the electronic platform. For now, focus on the *what* and *why* of this work for them and for you. The *what* for them is to give and receive feedback. The *what* for you is to see how your new students handle this step in the process. The *why* for them is to see what classmates are writing and to learn what the writers can do better as they revise before submitting their stories for assessment/grading, The *why* for you is to get better-written narratives that won't take so long to read and grade.

For this first R.A.G. experience, (1) have students write their names on the rubric and lay it on top of their drafts. (2) One student from each group collects all the drafts and hands them to you.

(3) You distribute the drafts to other groups so that no one is reading the paper of anyone else in their group (Group A gets Group B papers, Group B gets Group C papers, etc.). This way, students are less likely to be distracted by watching how classmates respond to their paper. (4) During the R.A.G.,

each student reads five or six papers, but (5) responds to only two. Do not allow those without a draft to sit in on a R.A.G. Consider using FLIP-GRID as an option for students to give oral feedback to their peers.

Fairness suggests that paperless students sit out and use the time to work. First, it is useful to give those who are behind on their own writing class time to catch up. Second, if a student in a group does not have a paper to be read each round, then someone else has to "sit" out because of too few papers.

No need to worry about students coming unprepared the next time. Most are ready for the next R.A.G. because they want to see what others have written and also want to get feedback and suggestions for their own revisions. Curiosity is a great motivator.

Once the groups are formed and have their stack of papers, (1) the group leader distributes the drafts to group members, and (2) you set a timer for 3 minutes, which usually is enough time to read the two or three pages of these early drafts. (3) Students read the first paper until the timer goes off, then pass the paper to the right and read the second paper, the third paper and fourth until the timer goes off again. (4) After the fourth pass, set the timer for 6 minutes.

Next, (5) the students read and comment on the content of the paper. On the fifth pass, again, set the timer for 6 minutes; the students read and comment on the organization and style.

(6) Then, students write one sentence of commendation and one sentence with a recommendation for that classmate to consider during revising.

By this time, the students have learned

- a great deal about their classmates.
- ways their peers have responded to the prompts.
- problems that arise when one makes mechanical, usage, grammar, and spelling errors; and, equally enlightening.
- the quality of the pool of writing in which their own papers are to be read.

While students are reading the first two or three drafts, you can walk around the classroom and record in your grade book a check for the students who have their drafts ready on this due date. Afterward, during the longer reading times, you have a few moments to confer with those who have come unprepared; offer suggestions to get them back on track with their writing.

At the end of the R.A.G. session, each leader collects the group's papers and hands them to you. Before returning the papers and rubrics to the students who wrote them, spend 5 or 6 minutes soliciting from the class the strengths—using terms from the rubric—they noticed in the papers and invite suggested strategies for improving them. No need to mention weaknesses at this time.

Hand the papers to the writers and direct them to read the comments from their peers and then to write three steps the writer will take to revise the written narrative. Have the timer ring 5 minutes before the end of the period so you can summarize the experience and give the homework assignment.

Students can be assigned to email their revision plan to you within 24 hours. This email creates a record that the students have received feedback and have outlined a plan for revising. These stated plans can be a starting point when you begin reading the final papers and note whether the writers implemented their plans.

Assign the students to have their final drafts ready for you after two class meetings. During the intervening days, schedule in-class writing time for students to work on their revisions. If your students meet just once a week, do this R.A.G. assignment during the second segment of the class meeting, then, after their break, have students begin revising during the final segment of the class.

Do not feel frustrated if you find yourself adjusting the length of time needed for revision. Ask the students. Thankfully, students become personally invested in these papers and want you to see their best work. Do both them and yourself a favor—create a schedule that is flexible enough to allow them to revise. Well-written papers are a pleasure to read and take less time to grade.

If you teach in a setting where it is unrealistic to expect students to word process the final drafts at home, allot additional class time for students to use school equipment. Especially in writing, it is more important that students complete a few assignments well than to rush through lots of assignments that they cannot finish carefully and turn in with pride. This name-writing narrative is one to which they usually are willing to devote time. The subject, after all, is the students themselves.

On the due date, students should submit for evaluation a packet or upload a folder that includes their first drafts, the rubric with their plan, and the final copy on the top. This stack of papers or folder substantiates that the process of writing is a lot of work. If students have worked totally online and have done online peer reviews instead of R.A.G.s, then students should save and submit all drafts in their student folder that you can view online. See subsequent chapters for different configurations for online peer-response sessions.

Considering a Human-Interest Story

Another engaging way to invite students to write narratives or articles is based on their content major, the special license or certification they seek to earn in college. The prompt is simple and can include some basic research leading to their composing a newspaper article relating an imaginary event during which they are honored by their profession. The writing prompt is

With what prestigious award will you be honored in twenty years?

- Introduction—Who, what, when, where, why, and how about the award ceremony.
- Body Paragraphs
  - Education and career of the winner (you in twenty years).
  - Others who have won the honor in the past.
  - Ways this year's winner (you) compares to former winners.
- Conclusion—When and where the award will be given next year.

After revising and editing your article, add a recent photo of yourself.

Valuing the Writing Process to Learn about Students

These steps in the process of drafting a paper are important for new college classroom teachers, individual writers, and their classmates. Scheduling this assignment early in the course allows you to observe how students handle various steps in the writing process. You can expect them to be able to take these steps with relative independence by the second half of the term. Based on what you observe in the opening two or three weeks, you can design or adapt lessons appropriate for learning with students in each of your classes.

As the students exchange feedback during the interim stages of writing, they see how peers are addressing the assignment. For many students, this is both a comfort and a challenge. When they see that they and their peers are having similar problems, they do not feel so odd or incompetent. On the other hand, when they see how well some of their peers are doing, individual students realize that the task is possible, and they are challenged to work a little harder to meet the assignment standards.

Building on Prior Knowledge

Your students may be new to college but are not new travelers along the road of life. They are joining you for just this portion of a lifelong journey of living and learning. As a new college instructor or GTA/GSI you are both a fellow traveler and tour guide.

You have the responsibility to do all you can to prepare them for the weeks and months ahead, perhaps warning them of possible landslides that can occur and inclement weather they may experience, always assuring them that you are in this together. You are there to help them climb the rock walls of new tasks that seem unscalable; to work with them, eager to observe them open their hearts and minds to see and appreciate the beauty of reading, writing, and discussing culturally relevant issues and employing ethical use of rhetorical devices.

You will help them think about new kinds of writing, novel narratives, and fascinating essays, readying them to explore natural wonders encountered along the way. Most of all, you will guide their practice and use of skills as they strive to achieve their personal goals, achieving success in any content area or field of study.

CONCLUSION

Seriously consider a narrative writing unit as an efficient way to blend reading and writing that helps establish a nurturing environment in which students can be both vulnerable and supportive. Names and plans for the future reveal much about who and whose we are, where we have been, and where we might want to be going. What we plan for the future guides what we are doing today. Your carefully designed interactive instruction can help your students be prepared for almost any career path they choose to follow because communicating clearly is a benefit in any setting. See the companion website for this book, https://planningwithpurpose.info/, for more specific ways to adapt your teaching in a virtual community of learners.

NOTES

1. Oscar Hammerstein, "Getting to Know You," Sound Track Lyrics, accessed March 6, 2020, http://www.stlyrics.com/lyrics/thekingandi/gettingtoknowyou.htm.
2. Council of Writing Program Administrators, "WPA Outcomes Statement for First-Year Composition (3.0)."
3. Ralph Ellison, "Hidden Name Complex Fate," In Shadow and Act (New York: Random House, Inc, 1964), 148.

Chapter 3

Understanding Grammars to Negotiate Conventions

It is no longer an advantage to speak English, but a requirement! Just speaking English isn't so impressive anymore—unless you speak it really well.[1]

—Heather Hansen

Language is a glorious art, a phenomenal means of communication, and linguistic diversity is a gift to humankind. At the same time, there are always more formal, mainstream versions of languages that symbolize what it means to be educated. Furthermore, some career practitioners expect the use of certain syntactical patterns of those who walk that path. Skillful use of languages can lead to success in the workplace and in society in general.

In its position statement on language, power, and action, the Conference on College Composition and Communication (CCCC) states that "language is powerful. It empowers individuals to explore and change themselves and their world. A belief in this power of language and the abilities of writers to ethically use language is a core principle of CCCC."[2] This chapter explores reasons that new college instructors and graduate teaching assistants (GTAs) can incorporate discussions of culturally sensitive grammar and writing into instructional practices.

In a diverse world full of different idiolects and dialects, students increasingly need to know how languages work so they can "code-switch" and "code-blend" in personal, professional, and public life. Think about ideas in this chapter as you plan lessons that help raise awareness of grammar—that set of rules that govern the structure of oral and written speech.

The Council of Writing Program Administrators (CWPA) Outcomes Statement notes that "successful writers understand, analyze, and negotiate conventions for purpose, audience, and genre."³ Integrating grammar activities can help students understand the value of knowing when to use what many call Standard English grammar to achieve academic and professional success. Students also thrive when they understand the jargon and vocabulary of specific content areas. What style should students be learning to be successful in the content areas you are teaching?

CONSIDER THE IMPACT OF STANDARD ENGLISH WITH ANNA'S STORY

The occasion to demonstrate the value of speaking Standard English occurred when a friend invited me to present in a community project which taught high school students tutoring skills necessary in after-school programs. Prior to my visit, my friend had sung my praises. She had told students I was an experienced teacher who had also had a successful sales career. Student expectations were high.

I arrived, dressed casually, and quietly sidled into the classroom without saying a word until I was introduced. Then I began speaking in slang, using street vernacular similar to the dialect of that community. The students looked at each other askance, puzzled that my pre-established ethos did not match the image I conveyed in my attire, posture, and speech. After fumbling with my papers, I blurted, *"Oh darn it! I cain't find my notes!"*, then fled the room as if to retrieve them.

The students erupted with comments to each other and questions to my friend. *"She don't sound like a teacher, do she?" "I thought you said this woman is educated!" "She don't look like it!" "Where you get her from?" "Teachers ain't supposed to sound like that!"*

My friend let the students talk for a few minutes. After I removed the vest that clashed with my blouse and straightened my skirt, I reentered the room with notes in hand. I walked more erectly to the front of the room, addressed students in Standard English, and invited them to repeat their first impressions of me.

When asked why they were surprised and even disappointed in my appearance and speech, students acknowledged the disconnection between their preconceptions and my presentation. They admitted that, based on their teacher's description of my educational background and experience, they had expected me to speak *"better"* English. They soon grasped that just as they had made assumptions about me based on my clothing, grammar, and articulation, others could make the same assumptions about them. Point made.

The form of English that one knows and uses is important. The way one speaks and writes Standard English makes a difference in the way one is perceived by others. These students witnessed firsthand the practical value of code-switching and were ready to practice another way of speaking. Lesson learned.

CHOOSE THE APPROPRIATE GRAMMAR

Few students and not all teachers use perfect grammar, but both groups recognize when others speak or write in ways that do not adhere to rules of Standard English. Even though you and your students may come from backgrounds with linguistic variations, students generally expect learned prose to sound the same—formal and in the dialect heard from national television broadcasters that tends to be based on the Midwestern pronunciations.

Students see college as a place for speaking and writing in more formal dialect and syntax, not necessarily in the communication style of the world students may experience outside the classroom. The (CCCC) advocates honoring the language of students. Note that "while the CCCC National Language Policy supports English as the language of wider communication, it protects the civil rights of speakers of all languages and language varieties, in the hope of contributing to greater linguistic, ethnic, and racial respect and justice in our multiethnic, multicultural society."[4] We urge you to do the same.

For those students who did not grow up hearing Standard English, a college is a place where this different language is spoken, read, and written. This reality is a good reason to teach English dialects the same way English speakers are taught languages like Arabic, French, or Spanish. In order to encourage speaking the specific language, some instructors tell students that once they cross the threshold of the classroom, they are to communicate only in the language they are learning. This is pretty drastic for an introductory college class but worth considering in a modified form.

Of course, when students talk among themselves in small groups, there is no need to stop them from speaking their dialects. But in a full-class discussion, urge them to code-switch or code-blend and incorporate as much Standard English as possible. This practice can serve them well outside the classroom when they find themselves in situations where it is personally or professionally advantageous for them to speak Standard English.

Students become amenable to grammar lessons when they learn that you are teaching them a form of speaking and writing that is useful to them not only in your class but also beyond the community of college into their career, business, and civic lives. True, Standard English is not all there is to the real world. Still, it is essential for students of all linguistic backgrounds to learn when, where, why, and how to switch among linguistic variations.

The real issue is not who speaks or writes "properly" but instead how well someone can communicate effectively in various settings. Because most students understand this, you do not need to avoid the issues of language, culture, power, and privilege. Use the issues as teaching topics that hit home, even for those from superficially homogeneous communities.

Figure 3.1 Analyze the Work of Published Authors. What Works? *iStock/DMEPhotography.*

In his reflection, José Luis Cano, one of our contributors, wrote about his first year teaching in a community college in southern Texas. He described a multimodal activity that he used with his bilingual Spanish-speaking students:

> I assigned this project toward the end of the semester because . . . students had built a familiarity with concepts in rhetorical theory, and they were used to us discussing certain terms, namely *"audience."* . . . this particular assignment . . . made use of a linguistic dexterity that most students possess and imagines an entirely different audience than an academic one, yet students who felt uncomfortable could still create the poster in English-only.
>
> In groups of two or three, I asked students to identify a refrán or dicho (a proverb or words of wisdom) . . . they had to write it out on a poster/canvas, which a Spanish speaking/reading audience would understand. They also had to create a visual on the poster which would convey the same message for non-Spanish speaking audience . . . For example, one poster read, *"No todo lo que brilla es oro"* (not everything that shines is gold). The visual component included a sketch of a golden poop, which I found comical. In other words, the refrán/dicho cautions against falling for situations that seem too good at first but may end up being otherwise.

I expected some resistance about using Spanish in a composition course, but only a handful of students decided to write their words of wisdom in English. This comfort toward this bilingual assignment probably stemmed from my insistence on bringing in the external community as an audience throughout the semester. This approach probably translates well to areas . . . where linguistic diversity exists. Next time, I'd have to reconsider if I want to include a digital option for a poster . . . This assignment . . . used the linguistic and community knowledge that students possess and seldom appears in the college classroom. As a bilingual educator, I thoroughly enjoyed knowing that I was developing students' full scope of rhetorical agility.

HONOR LA DIFFÉRENCE

Inevitably the issues of dialects in written and media texts arise when teachers require that students use Standard English in their assignments. Some may get the impression that instructors disrespect students' native tongues or linguistic variations—even students' multi-linguistic competence. Who says that Standard English is more academic, more worthy of being taught?

Invite your students to ask their classmates (or, outside of class, friends, and family members) about the experiences they have had with language. Often their stories substantiate your claims better than anything else. Consider reading and talking about the poem "The Phone Booth at the Corner" by Juan Delgado, which relates such a situation. Since few students are familiar with phone booths, you may need to show them pictures of red telephone boxes that often are seen in contemporary British movies.

Proficiency in speaking and writing Standard English is the ticket to career advancement in many professions. For this reason, educators have the responsibility to help students acquire this language while honoring students' heart or heritage languages, the language with which they are most comfortable and consider their own. By so doing, effective teachers model what it means to respect others' languages and cultures.

An article in the May 2020 edition of *California English*, the professional journal of the California Association of Teachers of English, advocates "translanguaging." This pedagogical approach grants students the option not only to code-blend, using various dialects of English, but also to mingle multiple languages when doing so enhances communication. After all, the goal in communication is to transmit messages from the composer to a target audience of readers, viewers, or listeners.

In the ancient world, honoring others was the basis for hospitality—making room for the "stranger" who is different from us and our culture. You can teach and honor the students by respecting their ability to communicate effectively in their own codes. When you do this, you may realize that you also are a stranger. Why? Because one's standard grammar and mother tongue are different than the linguistic norms of others. By practicing linguistic hospitality, students and teachers learn what it is like for others to be strangers, and all come to recognize one's own "strangeness."

LET AUTHORS AND SPEAKERS MODEL FOR YOU

Showing students ways that published authors and media communicators use dialect to create valid and interesting presentations is another reason to include model texts and video clips.

Later, when students focus on their own composing while also thinking about others' work, impatient students become more conscientious about revising their own work. They realize they have to think about their audiences: readers, viewers, listeners, and especially about communicating as authentically and respectfully as possible, then recognize they must get it right on behalf of the people they are writing about, not just for themselves.

Some students, inspired by what they read and view, decide to incorporate dialect or syntax that reflects the oral language of a specific ethnic group or

Figure 3.2 Remind Students to Adjust Lingo for the Intended Audience. *iStock/monkeybusinessimages.*

geographical region. If others can do it, students reason, why can't they? Why shouldn't they at least try? By all means, give them the freedom to do so. But your students need to know that it is easy to offend those for whom a dialect is their own. The easiest place to start is writing within one's own dialect. Even then, here is the key: students need to understand that when they write in their own voice—the voice of the linguistic group with which they identify—they are making a choice with consequences for themselves as well as their readers.

Fortunately, many students are already learning some code-switching and code-blending by writing for digital media. They learn "texting" on a cell phone or tweeting online. They learn that writing blogs is somewhat similar to journaling. Some write "fan fiction" on popular websites, trying to imitate their favorite writers. In other words, college students tend to be published code-switchers already even if they do not think of Facebook, Instagram, SnapChat, or Twitter and other social networking websites as "publications" with their own styles and rules. Moreover, whether they like it or not, students realize others are interpreting and evaluating what and how they write.

CONCLUSION

New college teachers, GTAs, and GSIs like you, are called on to teach many grammars of code-switching and code-blending, using words and images in text, audio and verbal, print and digital media. The task is not to promote particular cultures or languages over others but to make sure that students are competent in Standard English and develop the basic ability to move among the idiolects, learning to blend them when appropriate.

You are called on to show the appreciation of your students' languages as well as the particular language arts skills you bring. You do this because you recognize that knowing and understanding language is practical. Language is an art as well as a skill, a means for human beings to be able to understand and be understood, to serve others, and be served by them. Language is at the center of who we are as cultures, nations, communities, religious groups, and more. Specific styles are key to success in specific careers. Teach that, too.

Studying language as it is written and spoken helps students understand communication and practice it more ethically and effectively. It is primarily through visual and verbal language that students start understanding what separates people and what unifies them. Honoring linguistic abilities is a major component of honoring those shared differences. Through the lessons you design, you show students that all humans share this amazing ability to switch codes in the midst of the very differences that confuse and divide people.

As an educator, you can model respect, thus teaching your students to honor differences. And when students question why a "great" author can break the rules while a student might be viewed as inept or is marked down for using the same nonstandard code, the answer is straightforward: students need to be able to switch from one to another linguistic variation depending on the setting. Most college writing across the content areas is the setting for using Standard English.

NOTES

1. Heather Hansen, "Speak English Clearly and Grammatically, and Boost your Success!," accessed April 3, 2020, https://www.streetdirectory.com/travel_guide/191314/phones/speak_english_clearly_and_grammatically_and_boost_your_success.html.

2. Conference of College Composition and Communication, 2016, "Statement on Language, Power, and Action," Last modified November 2016, accessed April 20, 2020, https://cccc.ncte.org/cccc/language-power-action.

3. Council of Writing Program Administrators, "WPA Outcomes Statement for First-Year Composition (3.0)."

4. Conference of College Composition and Communication, "Statement on Language, Power, and Action."

Chapter 4

Writing to Clarify Thinking

Writing organizes and clarifies our thoughts. Writing is how we think our way into a subject and make it our own. Writing enables us to find out what we know—and what we don't know—about whatever we're trying to learn.[1]

—William Zinsser

Writing is a means of expressing, exploring, and expanding our understanding. Those who teach in any content area can tap into this powerful neurological experience to enhance the learning of the teacher about the students and the students about their subject. According to research conducted during the pursuit of a Master of Arts degree, it became clear to Anna how important it is for students to write about their experiences learning. If they are not writing in their own words in the first weeks of a course, by the end of the year, students can experience retention loss of more than three-quarters of what they were taught!

Amazing research like this compels teachers in all content areas to consider ways to incorporate a range of writing opportunities into their lessons. As you mull over whether this practice is worthwhile, know that writing in and of itself is a heuristic, a way of knowing. Furthermore, one of the Writing Program Administrators (WPA) Outcomes Statements says that students should be learning to use "composing and reading for inquiry, learning, critical thinking, and communicating in various rhetorical contexts."[2] As students search for words to express themselves, they are thinking about what they know and are able to do.

To be beneficial, writing for this purpose does not have to be collected, read, or graded. It can be used as preparation for talking about newly taught concepts and reflecting on ones being practiced. On the other hand, on quizzes and tests, when teachers include questions requiring students to explain how to solve problems, writing can be graded for clarity and accuracy. This kind of writing-to-learn to clarify thinking works equally well in math, science, engineering, social sciences, art, music, and other courses as it does in English composition and oral communication classes.

The benefit of assigning writing-to-learn is threefold: expressive/exploratory writing activities increase the confidence and competence of students taking the course. This kind of writing also provides an ongoing evaluation tool for assessing what students are learning without giving stressful tests or dealing with tedious grading assignments. The third value of adding writing-to-learn to your instructional practices brings your work in line with the WPA outcome goal on processes. The WPA document states that students in your classes should be learning how to "Reflect on the development of composing practices and how those practices influence their work."[3] This is a win-win-win for all.

Reading what students write helps college teachers to identify more quickly specific deficiencies and to measure the understanding of various content-specific concepts and their applications. Writing-to-learn clarifies thinking, stimulates metacognition and verbalization—both talking and writing—and encourages shared inquiry when you invite students to discuss and question their peers in collaborative/cooperative learning group activities.

Figure 4.1   Writing about Learning Deepens It. *iStock/monkeybusinessimages.*

SHOW HOW WRITING IS REVEALING

When and where should students do this kind of writing? Regularly write in their journals. In addition to their traditional class notes, students can

- record specific concepts they believe they learned after an in-class presentation or homework assignment;
- react to what they are learning or what they are assigned but not learning;
- explain how to read bibliographic entries, website URLs, graphs, charts, and maps in history/social science;
- explain how to perform specific procedures in math, science, art, or gym.

What do these kinds of assignments look like? The student samples are from a booklet "Writing-to-learn in Math: Collaboration/Cooperation—Learning Pairs and Groups," written for teachers interested in implementing this kind of writing-to-learn and clarify thinking. See companion website: https://planningwithpurpose.info/

UNDERSTAND WRITING TO EXPRESS, EXPLORE, AND DISCOVER

Expressive writing occurs when students put into words what they think they are learning and is very much like speech. Such writing usually is uncensored for grammatical correctness and intended to communicate with the writer, not with the teacher/reader. The students put into their own words their understanding of a recently taught concept, and also how they feel about what they are learning. (The following examples are from math students, but you get the idea.)

10/28
Dear Journal:

My first C!! Boy did I bomb this baby! My mistakes are mostly careless and since I didn't get time to check it, they couldn't be corrected. Some of the word problems were misinterrupted [sic] and so my answers weren't checked out. The exponent mistakes were just stupid!

—EM

Exploratory writing helps students figure out how to solve certain procedures. Exploratory writing can be assigned in any course to have students show they know the correct way to cite resources in the college-required format. So, it is much better to discover this skill early, before that ream of research papers comes in for grading.

9/28

$3(x5) = 1/5(10x25)$ You should distribute 3 and 1/5 to the numbers. Then you would get the ex's to the left and the 3's to the right. Then you should simplify and solve. Ones I can't do are $c- 2y=b$. I cannot understand this! Which variables do you solve? How could you do it? I don't UNDERSTAND!!!! I was trying to solve for Yb instead of just solving. I missed what the book said.

Discovery writing is the kind of writing students do when they analyze and figure what they know about the various assignments they are given. In assignments like this, students look carefully at the kind of errors they made on specific assignments and then write what they discovered about their own work.

10/28

Dear Journal:

I could of done better on the test. I got two wrong on the exponents which I knew how to do but forgot. I made one silly error on Sci. Not (Scientific Notation) by forgetting it was a negative (insert 10 (–4 exponent). One part I did not know the difference between of % and more than % and on the chemical prop I set it up right but worked it out wrong. And I messed up on the age problems. Now I know to stick with the first answer.

—BA

You probably notice that the student entries include elements of multiple kinds of writing: expressive, exploratory, and discovery. This will be true of the writing-to-learn and clarify thinking your students do, too. To be most useful, assign this kind of writing early in the course, and continue doing so on a regular basis.

Part of the value of expressive/exploratory/discovery writing is the fluency that develops once students are used to it. They begin to look forward to the opportunity to unravel their thoughts and be prepared to ask focused questions for clarification from you and from their peers.

CLARIFY TEACHING AND FOCUS STUDY

Consider adapting ideas from this series of activities to maximize your students' learning experience. Periodically giving homework assignments that require students to explain how they solve problems can elicit strong evidence of their understanding. You find yourself preparing with more care and clarity as you think about what you will ask students to know well enough to write at the beginning, middle, and end of the course.

Students respond to these writing-to-learn assignments by paying attention to their reading, viewing, and in-class activities because they know they will be asked to articulate their understanding in their own words. Students begin to

- focus on their assignments and performance;
- analyze reasons for the success or failure in the subject;
- reflect on what they read in their text and experience in class;
- verbalize more comfortably in written and oral forms with you and their classmates; and
- collaborate more confidently because they already have begun thinking and finding words to express themselves more precisely.

Of course, none of these outcomes is isolated. A student may focus and analyze during a reflection and verbalize during a collaborative situation. Your goal is to understand and design writing and speaking assignments that enhance the teaching and learning experiences in your classroom.

OBSERVE WAYS STUDENT TALKING TEACHES

Combining writing activities with talking in collaborative pairs, triads, and small group discussions enrich the learning experience. Once students have written their thoughts about what they are learning or not learning, they have words to talk about it with peer partners and in whole-class discussion. As you circulate around the classroom—observing, listening, and peeking over their shoulders at what the students have written—you can quickly determine what students know or still find confusing and adjust the lesson to meet the current state of their learning, comfort or discomfort.

Include opportunities in virtual settings for students to talk to one another verbally and in writing in the vocabulary of your content areas. Practice may not make them perfect, but practice will make students more confident.

GROUP STUDENTS IN PAIRS, PODS, AND SMALL GROUPS

Vary the kind of writing you assign based on the lessons you are teaching. For example, if students have had what you know has been a challenging homework task, begin the next class assigning an "admit slip" on which students write a sentence or two in which they admit or acknowledge what proved difficult for

Figure 4.2 Collaborating Enriches the Learning Experience. *iStock/SeventyFour.*

them to understand or do. Ask them to be specific and refer to the section or page of the handout, text, or video. Then ask students to pull their desks or chairs together so they can work in pairs, using their six-inch voices to discuss the question/problem and try to come up with a response using class notes or their textbooks. Or, in a virtual setting, assign them to virtual rooms.

Another time, while presenting a particularly complex lesson, stop and ask students to write a summary. For this, they can write three or four sentences in their own words about what they are hearing:

- A definition of a concept
- A summary of what they have learned so far
- A question they have about what has been presented or viewed

Allow a few minutes for several students to read aloud what they have written. These readings can reinforce the value of writing while revealing whether or not the students are grasping the ideas being presented. Frequently students will phrase the definition in words more familiar to their classmates and more easily understandable than those in the formal definition, academic, or content-specific vocabulary you may have used.

In another setting, it may be valuable to have students answering peers' questions themselves. Collect the slips and redistribute them to students on the opposite side of the room. Give the students a minute or two to read the slips to see if they can resolve the issue themselves. It may take a few times of working this way for students to stay focused on a task. If they get off task, immediately stop the session and have students return desks and chairs to the regular format. In virtual settings, have students post and respond in chats.

Some GTAs collect from one group or pod and distribute to another across the room and have the groups work together to answer the questions. Either way, gets students thinking, reflecting, and working together—all keys to your own good teaching.

It may take a couple of weeks for them to be comfortable with this kind of vulnerability. As you cultivate trust in them and model courteous commenting, the students soon follow your lead. When they get off the task, gently call attention to the front and go on with the lesson of the day, using the admit or summary slips to guide your instruction for the remainder of the class time.

The next day, allot just a little less time for paired talking; then on subsequent days, extend the time in half-minute increments until you reach 4 to 6 minutes. Circulating around the classroom helps maintain order and provides opportunities to listen, observe, and redirect attention as necessary. Students will come to value this time to figure out answers and clarify their thinking.

The exit slip can be used in a similar way. About 5 to 7 minutes before the end of the period, distribute 3 × 5 cards or pieces of scrap paper to each student. If they are working on computers, have them send you a message on a texting app designed for classrooms like TwitterChat and Google Classroom. Ask students to write in their own words what you taught that period and what they have learned and may be able to use in your course or another one.

Again, content, not form, is important in these notes. Merely collect these anonymous notes as students leave the classroom. Reading them later will give you a better idea of what concepts the students have grasped and which need further clarification before proceeding on to new material. Just remember to set a timer to ring 5 minutes before the official end of class, so there is time to access the apps, write and send the exit slip before students have to pack up and leave. The timestamp will show when the email was sent.

All three—the admit, summary, and exit slips—are effective ways for both student and instructor to learn. If the students can find the words to write fairly clearly what they know, they know they know; if they can't, they know that, too, and can either ask for help or study themselves. They do not have to wait until a graded assignment to learn what they know. This kind of writing helps show who knows what, now.

WRITE THE STEPS

The comforting activity, Write the Steps, is a version of the summary sentence and can work well in math, science, physical education, music, or art class. After explaining a new procedure for an important process in your class, have students write in order, in their own words, the steps to completing that task. It could be solving a math problem, setting up a lab, calling a foul, tuning an instrument, preparing a piece of clay before throwing on the wheel, or gathering information and writing citations for different resources required for a research paper.

Ask the students to turn and talk to a partner or group about the steps they wrote. As the steps are read, all can listen to these versions and can hear various ways of stating the procedure. Take time to clarify cloudiness or confusion. Resist the temptation to force students to use formal language if what they have written is correct.

Somehow, this Write the Steps activity can be a reassuring exercise for the class. All can hear how classmates are thinking/not thinking and recognize that they are not alone in getting/not getting the new material. At the same time, you can monitor and adjust as needed. By writing the steps, the students can focus and reflect, figure out, and clarify their thinking under your guidance, thus advancing the learning for more students in less time.

ASSIGN REFLECTIVE WRITING: IT'S VALUABLE EVEN IF UNCOMFORTABLE

After a particularly challenging assignment, you could ask students to analyze that experience by responding to such prompts as the following:

- What task or kind of writing was most difficult for you—one that you are proud you have been able to complete on time?
- What task or step in the writing process is still difficult for you to do well?
- Try to describe the errors or kind of errors you made most often.
- What circumstances made it difficult for you to do better on this assignment?

The purpose of this informal writing assignment is to gain insight into students' thinking about the learning, not to measure the accuracy of their grammar, spelling, punctuation, and sentence structure. If you understand what they are saying, there is no need to use that red pen to circle or deduct credit for such minor errors. No comments save grading time, too.

Through the post-assessment reflections, instructors gain insight into students who have test anxiety, those who may be home alone regularly, those who had little time to study because they had multiple out-of-class demands on their time or energy, and those whose English comprehension skills may make it difficult for some to comprehend the assignments as written. Such specific details can help address issues with students and those raised by professors and department administrators who are overseeing your work as a new college teacher or graduate teaching assistant.

Figure 4.3 Reading What Students Write Gives Insight into What They Think. *iStock/fizkes*.

ANALYZE ASSIGNMENT AND TEST PERFORMANCE

It takes some students years to learn how to take tests and how to learn from the kinds of mistakes they make, so allot a full-class meeting to go over tests or reflect on comments from their major paper when you return them. What kind of topics should you cover during such an analysis? First, ask students to determine the kinds of errors they made. See sample questions in table 4.1.

Table 4.1 Analyze Assessment Results

1. I am pleased that _____
2. I am surprised/disappointed that _____
3. My grade is lower because of (mark appropriate reasons)
   - misread instructions
   - careless errors
   - inaccurate not enough details
   - incomplete answers
   - wrong material studied
   - other (explain)
4. This grade accurately/inaccurately reflects what I earned on this assignment. ____ Yes ____ No. Why? /Why Not? . . .
5. Based on this analysis, I see my strengths are
6. On the next assignment, next semester, I must focus . . . .

Once students determine the kinds of errors they made, talk about ways to avoid them next time. Usually, students calm down when they learn that correcting one problem before the next test can help them lose fewer points the next time. Some GTAs ask students to come to one-on-one conferences with the responses to the questions the students have written. Those written responses can focus and guide the time together and help both the new college instructor and the student plan ways to proceed.

CONCLUSION

Combining writing-to-learn activities with collaborative talking is an efficient way to use class time. Once students have responses written in their own words and then turn and talk with their partners, they often can resolve problems on their own. This concurrent learning is less time consuming than your answering all their questions one by one. As you circulate among them, listening and observing, you learn right away what needs more instruction and time for practice or what is clearly understood and, therefore, can be tested with confidence.

Consequently, if you are among those who are reluctant to add writing-to-learn in classroom practices, you can relax. Unless the question is part of a test, this is ungraded writing. It is designed for you and your students to process what is taught and being learned. Reading what students write provides a window into their understanding, which, as a no-stress formative assessment, effectively guides you in future lesson planning. Being asked to write helps students know what they know and how to zone in on what they do not know . . . yet.

NOTES

1. William Zinsser, GOODREADS (2020), accessed March 6, 2020, https://www.goodreads.com/work/quotes/572323-writing-to-learn#:~:text=.
2. Council of Writing Program Administrators, "WPA Outcomes Statement for First-Year Composition (3.0)."
3. Ibid.

Chapter 5

Engaging Expository Writing

People are usually more convinced by reasons they discovered themselves than by those found out by others.[1]

—Blaise Pascal

Writing is a personal way to express oneself. While purpose determines the rhetorical mode one uses, arrangement, length, style, and vocabulary remain the choice of the writer. Unfortunately, many first-year college teachers experience what Jessica Hudson describes, "students don't see themselves as real writers, only as students taking a required GenEd class. For the most part . . . they don't believe they have a promising voice or a perspective worth writing from." The challenge for new college instructors is to create a learning environment in which these reluctant, even skeptical students begin to believe they can become effective writers in any content area.

This chapter describes ways to manage this quandary with suggestions for designing engaging lessons that inspire students to read and critique, research, then write and speak on topics of interest to them. Here are ideas that can help students meet goals outlined by the Council of Writing Program Administrators (CWPA) Outcomes Statement that says students should be "negotiating purpose, audience, context, and conventions as they compose a variety of texts for different situations,"[2] such as that of informing by writing expository essays.

In the college classroom, it sometimes is easy to lose sight of the ultimate goal of education—to help students acquire knowledge and develop the range of skills needed to live self-sufficient, productive lives in a pluralistic society. However, as instructors work backward, accepting that goal and planning lessons to help reach it, they learn to stay on track without becoming rigidly shortsighted. So, what does this have to do with teaching students how to compose expository essays?

It means remembering that our classroom is a training ground where we, like athletic coaches, introduce new information, demonstrate skills, and then schedule opportunities for students to practice reading, writing, and speaking. But finally, when the game begins, we trust our burgeoning writers to choose what works in the heat of the game—when they want to express themselves to others.

Writing outcome goals like those for your course generally require teachers to present a range of strategies for prewriting, revision, editing, and publishing that have proven to be effective for different kinds of writing and purposes. Successful educators somehow learn to do this without insisting that every student execute each step in the same way for every assignment. None works well for every writer every time. Ask the zillion published authors out there.

How, then, does one teach in light of this reality? Make plans guided by the college department standards and remain flexible. You may be handed a curriculum like one of our contributors noted. Shanika Carter, a recent new-to-community college instructor wrote, "At first, I actually did not mind having the curriculum all set for me to follow, as I was in the process of 'becoming' an instructor. I now appreciate the freedom to apply my own personal touches and experiences in the classroom." Until you reach this point, please note the ideas here to help you strategically plot a course for this part of the voyage.

No need to worry. You can navigate the tricky waters without fearing Scylla and Charybdis, those rocks and whirlpools that could distract you from effectively teaching composition and communication in your content area. Lessons that follow help you engage students to write engaging expository essays they enjoy writing and you enjoy reading.

CHOOSE JUST THE RIGHT RHETORICAL MODE FOR THE OCCASION

Expository writing calls for clear explanations or descriptions to inform a specific audience about a concept, process, or topic. Students know a lot and are learning more. Invite them to utilize the composing process to conduct basic research and write about a topic that is important to them. The focus may be a sport, a way to prepare a meal, to create a piece of art, or to take the temperature of an infant or senior citizen. For example, students have composed and presented expository essays as demonstration speeches during which they explained or showed us how to

- milk a cow,
- change a bicycle tire,
- make a tortilla,
- play a clarinet,
- use origami and fold a peace dove,
- mow the different lawns on a golf course!

The topic isn't important, but knowing the process to compose for an identified audience is. The students may augment their presentation with multimodal components such as slides or video, or use hand-held props to supplement the words they write and speak.

The five-paragraph essay is one of many structures your students may have been taught. It is a formula designed to encourage students to flesh out their writing by developing their position statements into meaty paragraphs. However, this prescriptive mode does not work well for some students, and it is seldom seen in professional publications. Therefore, rather than adhere strictly to a formula that can stifle writing, be flexible regarding the number of words, paragraphs, or pages for each assignment.

College instructors working with new-to-college students do better teaching about the parts of an essay—introduction, body, and conclusion—and the function, purpose, or responsibility of each of these parts. In other words, avoid hardlines regarding quantity. Instead, insist that the final essay include the necessary parts.

Seeing is believing. Next are some active physical and visual ways to create memorable metaphors to help your college students understand and remember key elements about organizing and developing engaging expository presentations. If you have a way to adapt any idea in a virtual setting, please share it on our companion website: https://planningwithpurpose.info/

ACT OUT AN ESSAY

How about calling on kinesthetics to help students understand the structure of an essay? You could invite the class to demonstrate an essay that has the three requisite parts. Jock Mackenzie, author of *Essay Writing: Teaching the Basics from the Ground Up*[3] recommends instructing students to organize themselves into an essay. The only requirement for the first step is to have at least three groups—to represent the introduction, the body, and the conclusion. This exercise may take a little time, so use your timer to help pace the steps.

- For the first step, set your timer for 5 to 7 minutes, depending on the number of students and the classroom space. Then step aside, listen, and watch

how students decide who should stand where and why. When the buzzer rings, ask students to freeze and look around.
- You could ask those in the introduction section to raise their hands; those in the section(s) for body paragraph(s) to raise their hands, and then those in the conclusion section to do the same.
- What are you looking to see? Proportion. Are there fewer students in the introduction and conclusion sections?

• Next, direct the subgroups to move into separate corners of the room. Each group—introduction, body, and conclusion—is to come up with a gesture or body pose to indicate the function of their part of the essay. Again, set the timer for 5 to 7 minutes; step aside, observe, and listen to what they do and say. What may you see?
- The introduction group may arrange themselves into a triangle with each member gesturing forward with his or her pointer finger to indicate the introduction shows the way the essay will go. One person may represent the thesis statement.
- The body group may arrange themselves into two or more smaller groups to indicate multiple paragraphs. Each subgroup may have one student representing the topic sentence.
- The conclusion group may stand and gesture "time-out" to indicate the essay is coming to an end. This group may arrange itself in a triangle and point their thumbs over their shoulders to indicate the conclusion may look back to point to what has already been developed in the body.

• Now, ask the students to demonstrate the need for transitions between sections and between sentences by reaching out and linking pinky fingers. Yes, they will giggle, but that's typical. Then, call a freeze, a pause for silence. Now, using the camera on your cell phone, snap a photo before directing students to return to their seats. In a virtual settings, just have students hold up their pinky fingers. They'll smile and think you're silly. But they will remember

• Close with a debriefing session reflecting on the choices they made and how their final tableau did, in fact, demonstrate the structure and process of writing an essay. Yes, they were confused at first, had to ask questions, and consider function to decide where to stand and how to organize themselves as a class. The same is true in the process of writing. It takes time to decide what to include and where to put details in an essay, too.

In the lessons to come, remind them of this exercise and maybe point to the photo of them on a slide you can project during class. This may feel silly to you as a GTA working with adults but try it anyway. Sometimes what we learn being silly stays in our minds. One thing you could say to challenge college students is, "You may have done this in middle school. Let's see how quickly you can do this as college students."

Engaging Expository Writing

Figure 5.1 Observe and Listen as Students Choose Topics. *iStock/Prostock-Studio.*

What is the pedagogical theory? Physical movement serves multiple functions in a learning environment that requires students to know and be vulnerable to one another. First, movement can release tension, increase blood flow, and motivate the brain. Talking to one another requires thinking and listening. Seeing and feeling what is happening creates memories that just may smooth the way to make students' writing better and your grading easier.

Equally important to you as the instructor is that observing and listening as students interact serve as formative assessments, helping you decide what needs to be modified in future lessons. You learn who the leaders are, who has the vocabulary for articulating traits of an essay, and who may be shy and needs your encouragement to get involved a little more.

INVITE STUDENT-CHOICE TOPICS FOR WRITING

A college course can be likened to a journey. An effective way to get to know the travelers on a journey is to invite them to write about what they know and expand that knowledge with guided research. Your student writers can pay attention to organization, sentence structure, and choice of language for the audience they identify for the composition. Use the same rubric, list of essay traits, as planned for this course, and customize for this assignment as suggested in chapter 1. See other ideas on your college department website.

Knowing the goals helps students meet the goals. Include mini-lessons to remind or show students how to select evidence from literary or informational texts to support analysis, reflection, and research as set forth in many composition course standards and CWPA Outcomes Statement goals.

Few college students are reluctant to write about what they know well, even in an unfamiliar classroom setting. Early writing designed to build community can nurture an environment that feels safe. Therefore, design assignments with the option to fictionalize details. One such narrative-expository assignment, described in chapter 2, asks students to think about their futures, the value of education, and the benefits of career planning.

DISCOVER AUTHOR'S PURPOSE AND RECOGNIZE ESSAY PATTERNS

Plan a lesson for students to discover or review the elements in the different modes of communicating. Encourage them to pay attention to the words as well as layout and graphics seen in multimodal print or online documents. Begin brainstorming, asking students to jot down three or four reasons people would want to communicate in the first place. Have them turn and share their lists with a partner on the left, then a partner on the right. Now call on speakers from four sections of the room—from a pair in the left back, right back, left front, then right front of the class. Write as they speak. The list should include the following purposes:

- to inform,
- to explain,
- to report,
- to argue,
- to persuade,
- to commemorate,
- to entertain.

Use the students' words at first to validate their contribution. You then, in later lessons, use the more formal or academic terms they may encounter in classes they take after this one.

SET UP THE DISCOVERY EXPEDITION

Check your textbooks or go online and gather five or six culturally relevant samples or mentor texts of different types of writing. No need to leave out humorous essays. They sometimes are more accessible and memorable. At this time, keep the reading short—just 300–500 words. For this hands-on activity, print and clip together five-six copies of each essay and acquire boxes of colored pencils for each table or group of five to six students. Pre-bundling materials reduces the time to distribute them during class.

TEXT BOX 5.1   CRITIQUING AN ESSAY FOR MODELING

Five W's and H Critique Write a three-sentence Summary for each of your chosen essays. Include answers to the 5Ws and H questions. Due by _____ 11 p.m.	*Who* is the author? *Who* is the audience? *What* is the title and a message? *What* is author's attitude (tone) about that topic or issue? *When* was the essay written? (Check the endnotes, footnotes, or bibliography?) *Where* was the essay published? (Check the endnotes, footnotes, or bibliography?) *Why* did you find this essay interesting? (Topic, language, length, other?) *How* will you use something you learned from reading this essay in your own next essay? (Style, organization, sentence structure, vocabulary? Other?)

Resist the temptation to rush the exploratory process by giving students clues ahead of time. Create slides with the step-by-step instructions so those who may not be paying attention can glance up, confirm they heard you right, and get back to work. Usually, one slide per step will suffice. Advance the slides to guide the class on to the next step. Have your timer set for 2 or 3 minutes, depending on the length or complexity of the writing and skill of your student readers. For virtual lesson, encourage students to set their own timers, then use color highlighting to complete the assignment.

- Distribute packets of essays and boxes of pencils.
- Advance to the first slide and set the timer for 2–3 minutes. (You can embed timer into slides.)
- Ask students to read silently and mark the paper when they notice what may be a clue to the kind of essay they have. (What are clues to the purpose of this essay?)
- Exchange pencils for a new color. Advance slide with instruction. This time read and mark what they recognize in terms of text structure and organization. (What transition words guide the writing and suggest organization patterns?)
- Exchange pencils once more, getting a third color. Advance slide. This time read and mark in the left margin symbols to indicate the beginning, middle, and end of one of the essays. Students may need 3–4 minutes for this task. (Use symbols to show the sections of the essay.)

- A triangle pointing down next to the beginning of the body section,
  - a rectangle where the middle or body begins,
  - a triangle pointing up to mark the start of the ending section.
- Finally, ask students to write what they think is the purpose of their sample essay: to inform, explain, compare, argue, persuade, commemorate, entertain, or whatever. Invite students to use emojis to show the purpose of the essay.

During these initial 12 to 15 minutes that students are working independently, circulate among them, paying attention to which students get right to work. Who seems to be puzzled and needs you to re-explain what they should be doing? Your physical proximity helps these intellectual investigators stay focused and to ask questions without attracting the embarrassing attention of their peers. (Remember to advance your slides showing what students should be doing for each reading.) As time permits, write anecdotal notes about what you observe regarding specific students and the class as a whole. Use the notes as you plan future lessons and activities.

After the last buzzer, have students confer for 3–5 minutes with others in their group to compare their findings. Some instructors invite students to write on poster paper or the classroom whiteboards to record, then share with the class what their group discovers. Again, set a timer for these "share outs" for 2–3 minutes. The goal is to provide the opportunity for students to mine their minds and share their thinking while you observe to determine what they already know and are able to do. What you learn will guide your preparation of the next assignments.

ACKNOWLEDGE MULTIPLE FEATURES IN ESSAYS

Be prepared for students to notice that essays often reflect multiple organizational patterns. Few pieces of writing reflect a single structure. Writers sometimes use narratives, telling stories, as they strive to persuade their readers. Some writers include descriptive passages when their primary goal is to report.

Invite student reporters to explain to the others how they labeled their sample(s) and what organization and text-structure clues helped them decide the purpose of their sample essay. As before, listen and observe to assess what they already know and what still needs clarification. Thankfully, students often are good teachers and save you valuable time by explaining the key points in ways their peers understand.

Finally, call the class together to merge their findings and to reflect on what they have discovered. How consistent are the findings? What characteristics do students notice in the different samples?

Later in the course, you may project two or three short sample essays and invite students to come forward and point to different parts, signal words, and other characteristics of the essay. Encourage them to use the academic language as much as possible. Or you may decide to have small groups work on the same essay and prepare and present a mini-lesson for the class. Remember, if you do it, you learn it; if they do it, they learn it. Yes, it's okay to repeat lessons using different essays. Just as in training for dance or sport, repeated exercising using different moves is key to polishing performances.

TAKE TIME FOR DISCOVERY

These discovery expeditions may take more than one class period or homework assignment. It's fine to repeat an activity if it is working. No need to rush. A practical follow-up assignment is to have students do this activity for homework. You can find websites like CommonLit.Org for free sets of readings with sample questions. No need to do all the gathering yourself; use what others have organized and posted for educators like you. Have students post their own responses to similar questions used in class.

Then during the next class meeting, reassemble the adventurers at the start of class to turn and talk about sample essays assigned for homework reading. Begin the next class meeting in groups in class or online to read and review what they discovered. You will have seen what they posted so have some idea where the discussions will go. After the independent and whole class experience with samples, the students are likely to have detected some of the patterns of organizing that you taught them to watch for when they are reading to learn and writing to inform:

- Description,
- sequential order,
- problem/solution,
- compare/contrast,
- cause/effect,
- directions,
- narrative, telling a story.

You can try to keep it simple at first but be prepared for students to notice that a writer may use one or more of these structures to fulfill any of the purposes for writing: to inform, to argue, to persuade, to entertain, and so forth. Therefore, you really are asking students to try to analyze and articulate (1) the purpose of the writing, (2) the use of text structures, as well as (3) the patterns of organization.

It also is likely that your discerning students may find it difficult to distinguish between the samples you may have included that illustrate argument and those that exemplify persuasion. You may have to point out, after such a comment, that argumentation presents opposing views and may add reasons for believing one side or the other, while persuasion usually includes a call for action or a plea to change one's belief or behavior.

DESIGN EXTRA CREDIT OPTIONS

By the second half of the course, students may become eager to do something extra to shore up a disappointing grade. If you have built into your syllabi this "Student Starter" option described in chapter 6, offer it now. In this case, students can practice what they are learning now and be better prepared for the major speaking assignment later in the course.

This extra credit option will help you measure how well they are meeting this CWPA outcome goal, "Develop facility in responding to a variety of situations and contexts calling for purposeful shifts in voice, tone, level of formality, design, medium, and/or structure."[4] Some instructors build extra credit choices. As mentioned in chapter 1, extra credit is only offered until the week BEFORE the final week of class. You do not need to be overwhelmed by an influx of extra work!

TEACH MORE THAN TELL

Yes, this kind of teaching will take more time than your giving a delightful lecture, showing a set of slides with definitions, or even labeling the writing samples and highlighting the different features for them; in that case, *you* will have done the thinking. More effective teaching and long-term retention occur when students seek out and find answers for themselves.

Effective teachers teach spirally, drawing earlier lessons into current ones, so students hear, see, and do enough to develop proficiency. In the long run, this could mean less reteaching by you or by those who teach the next course. What students discover for themselves, they remember.

Build in reteaching but with a twist. Plan multisensory lessons that require students to use physical as well as mental muscles like the earlier activity that asked for students to "act out an essay." Design lessons that have something for students to see, to hear, and to do each class meeting. Note recommendations for various pedagogically sound strategies as you continue reading this book.

Will you have to remind students of what they have seen, heard, and done? Of course. You very well may have some of these same students in higher-level classes and shake your head that they will have forgotten so much of what you thought you had taught so well. That probably is the main reason students have English classes the first two years in many majors in college. Not only because reading, writing, speaking, and listening form the basis for learning in most content areas, but also because students forget or see no immediate use for what they were taught earlier. If they do not use it, they lose it.

You, there in your role as an instructor or GTA, continue to provide multiple opportunities for students to exercise their skills, so their thinking muscles do not atrophy, making it difficult to use these muscles when they need them. Allotting time for students to write for real purposes creates engaging reasons to use expository modes to communicate.

That's where you are now! Ready to assign that expository essay in which the students are asked to inform a specific audience how to do something interesting. Now that students know their classmates better, these student writers can decide what they know well enough to explain or demonstrate to this audience.

For this expository assignment, the students

- identify an audience (veteran or novice);
- figure out what their audience needs to know to be able to do what the writer/speaker is explaining;

Figure 5.2 Known Classmates Can Now Be the Chosen Audience. *iStock/Prostock-Studio.*

- design multimodal components (props, slides, video) to help make this expository paper or presentation more engaging and effective;
- research to learn and incorporate historical background to help the audience understand the significance of this explanation or demonstration;
- cite those sources in the style required at your college;
- review the assignment grading rubric;
- experience the writing process that includes brainstorming, drafting, giving and receiving peer feedback, revising, then editing; and
- submitting an engaging expository composition for evaluation and grade as an essay or a multimodal oral presentation.

CONCLUSION

It may take several class sessions to cover the distance between reviewing expository writing to writing an effective essay and presenting an informative speech. Teaching and learning is a spiraling process in any content area. What they are trying themselves, students are likely to notice and point out during peer editing sessions. What they are discovering with your guidance is more lasting and useful than what they are simply shown or told about the specific subjects. What students prepare and share teaches them and their classmates. So, encourage students to record and post what they're learning on your class bulletin board. These short audio or video files will enhance the learning experience for you all.

You soon can move on to having students build on and synthesize the knowledge and skills learned while reading, critiquing, and developing written and oral communications. Students soon are ready to apply what you are teaching about engaging expository compositions to writing compelling arguments that show valid reasons members of an audience may hold various positions on controversial issues. The ability to compose engaging expository essays is a useful skill along any career path.

NOTES

1. Blaise Pascal, Brainyquote.com, accessed April 2, 2020, https://www.brainyquote.com/quotes/blaise_pascal_133403.
2. Council of Writing Program Administrators, "WPA Outcomes Statement for First-Year Composition (3.0)."
3. Jock Mackenzie, *Essay Writing: Teaching the Basics from the Ground Up* (Pembroke, NH: Pembroke Publishers, 2007).
4. Council of Writing Program Administrators, "WPA Outcomes Statement for First-Year Composition (3.0)."

Chapter 6

Composing Compelling Arguments

Build a firm foundation but don't get stuck.

An effective road to teaching students to write argumentative essays is to take time to build on skills students already have learned. Most college students have been writing reports since third grade, but some of your students may be multiple decades older now. It makes sense, then, to embark on this part of the trip by having your students practice writing short pieces before assigning an in-depth argumentative essay that requires sophisticated research.

You could ask them, "What are some of the reasons a person would want to write an argumentative essay?" Their answers are likely to include such things as to report, to explain, to describe, and to just share their feelings about a topic that may be controversial.

You probably have taught text structures, those organizational patterns that help guide a reader and reflect the purpose of the writing. See the sample review lesson in chapter 5. Now is the time to have students demonstrate what they understand about text structures by employing those devices in their own writing. On your class website, post documents with lists or links to some of the signal words—"because," "but," "for example," "however," "in conclusion"—used in published argumentative writing.

Kelsie Endicott, one of the new college teachers whose reflections guided our writing, acknowledged,

> The biggest mistake I made was that I failed to model reading strategies as in-depth or as frequently as I could have (in fact, I didn't even know much about reading strategies at that time, let alone how to teach them). I also didn't have students spend enough time practicing critical and close reading skills, and I didn't model the writing process for the argumentative essay as

comprehensively as I would've liked to. In short, I made the students aware of the reading strategies, but they weren't able to effectively employ them in their own reading due to poor modeling on my part and a lack of practice.

The suggestions that follow can help you through this process of planning class time, preparing lessons, and choosing activities that include ways to model and practice argumentative writing. When you can observe students using the skills you are teaching, you know they are learning. Then, you can be more confident that they can use these skills to complete homework assignments that include drafting, revising and editing their compositions. Again, consider the image of the coach planning and overseeing practice before the games that count.

BUILD THE FOUNDATION FOR CONVINCING ARGUMENTATIVE ESSAYS

For now, about halfway along the journey in the course, you know what students already can do, so now you can build on that knowledge. Have students draft a written argument about something they already know.

Figure 6.1　Build a Firm Foundation, but Don't Get Stuck. *iStock/monkeybusinessimages.*

Consider inviting your companions on this learning journey to explain why they believe it is important or interesting to know how to accomplish a task—build something, cook, sail, fish, rope a steer, ride a horse, pop an "Ollie" on their skateboard, or strategize in a board or computer game.

Your students may even choose to write about the value of the major they have chosen for college. Writing about their field of study is an excellent way to reinforce what your students are learning elsewhere, to validate the work of colleagues in other departments, and the value of English class for learning to write well. The varied topics for argument that your students choose create more interesting and compelling reading for you, too. If they can interest you about something new to you, it is likely the writing is compelling.

To reduce student temptation to copy from published work, begin the drafting of a one or two page argument in class. As students begin the required research, and before the final draft is due, remind them to cite their sources. Simple hyperlinking to the source in the draft of their essay can suffice for now. If they decide to keep this information in the final draft, students can use one of the online applications, like EasyBib or the feature in Microsoft Word, that create endnotes and bibliographies in the style used at your college. Hyperlinking can serve the same function as index cards used in twentieth-century classrooms.

As always, on a multi-draft assignment, students should date, save, and be able to show earlier drafts of their work. As they follow the assignment timeline, they and you can see how their writing evolves.

S.P.A.R. TO LISTEN FOR SOUND ARGUMENTS

Practicing aloud arguments and attempts to persuade is an effective way to prepare students for writing strong, convincing essays. Consider conducting S.P.A.R.s (spontaneous arguments) in class that are based on everyday topics, such as which is better, more nutritious, more popular, more useful, more economical, and more fun than something else. Students could S.P.A.R. about what should be required or banned.

For a S.P.A.R., two pairs of students debate one another for about 10 minutes per topic. They must include facts and not just opinions to be convincing. This is an exciting way to teach presenting, listening, and responding to opposing views on topics important to students of all ages and in culturally diverse discussions. Here are sample guidelines:

- Team A: Speaker 1 draws a topic from a hat or a bowl, announces it to the class, and then has just a couple of minutes to prepare and then present a case for making a change.

- Team B: Speaker 1, the opposing team, must address each argument presented by the first speaker and then within the 2 or 3 minutes counter each argument with his or her own.
- Team B: Speaker 2 then offers a rebuttal, or response, to those challenges.
- Team A: Speaker 2 sums up the arguments for Team B and calls for action.

The audience decides who presents the more convincing case by voting anonymously on a prepared ballot. Then the second set of students comes to the front, draws a topic, and presents their arguments and rebuttals. Usually, three rounds at a time are sufficient to demonstrate the value of listening and responding with logical reasons. The following is a structure that may help the S.P.A.R.ers.

- Name it: what's the problem or issue?
- Explain it: show why this is a problem or issue of concern for the audience.
- Prove it: use factual evidence, not just the opinion of the speaker.
- Conclude it: "Therefore . . ." State a good reason to consider the alternative view or to make a change.

Figure 6.2 Sound Reasoning, Not Volume, Convinces Audiences. *iStock/Deagreez.*

Students may notice how similar this is to the P.I.E. structure in developing paragraphs. The writers state their POSITION, offer ILLUSTRATIONS that ILLUMINATE—show and exemplify the position—and then EXPLAIN the link(s) between the two.

TAKE LOGICAL STEPS TO OTHER KINDS OF WRITING

The next logical step toward more complex writing would be to move on to a short compare/contrast assignment or speech for which students gather, organize, and write about two different people, places, things, events, or ideas. To keep this assignment concrete, again invite students to consider something they already know.

You could have them compare/contrast short essays they have read for your class and one they read on their own: a movie version versus print version of the topic; movies or television programs on the same topic; kinds of music; food; computer games; clothes; animals; cars, bicycles, boats, fishing rods, or saddles, a current event with one they read about in history or science. Consider a compare/contrast essay as an option for the major expository paper for your course. What are controversial topics in your content area?

Remind or show your budding writers two basic ways of organizing compare/contrast essays and invite them to use the pattern that works better for them. They could write the body of their paragraphs in blocks or stripes.

- Blocks
  - introduce the features to be considered
  - all comparisons or ways the topic being discussed are alike
  - all contrasts or ways the topic being discussed are different
- Stripes
  - feature of comparison 1—A and B together
  - feature of comparison 2—A and B together
  - feature of comparison 3—A and B together

The student's task, of course, is to decide what features or elements to compare or contrast. A Venn diagram is an effective graphic organizer for brainstorming and arranging the facts and explanations about how the two subjects of the essay are alike or different or are both alike *and* different. Writing a short compare/contrast essay may be a good opportunity to add multimodal elements. Students may hyperlink to a brief video or create a short set of slides to project during an oral presentation. What does the audience need to see or hear to better understand the reasons for the claim the writer/speaker is making?

For this basic compare/contrast essay, the students are simply reporting, but you may ask them to add an element of evaluation and state and explain which author the students think uses the elements more effectively; which product, song, or sport is better, or why fishing with one kind of rod is safer than another; which method is safer, more productive. Then the writers will be moving into argumentation, making a case for one story, product, behavior, or the other.

While it is okay to use "I think" and "I believe" in earlier drafts, ask the students to remove these phrases from the final draft. Just state their observations, and let those statements stand firmly on the reasons the student gives for taking such positions on the topic. Encouraging students to develop confidence in their supported assertions helps move them along into the more academic content writing required of them in subsequent college classes.

CONNECT WRITING TO CURRENT EVENTS

To keep the learning relevant, you could ask students to bring in samples from their reading that exemplify the kind of writing you are teaching. Locate, then link to two or three collections online of short argumentative and persuasive writing. Assign homework for which students choose one of each to bring to class. See CommonLit.org and other similar sites. It's okay to use less complex reading for these assignments. The goal is to show how professional writers use the strategies you are teaching.

In class, create groups of three or four students who have at least one of their chosen essays in common. Groups meet, choose the essay to analyze, mark the parts and create a 3–4-minute presentation of what they noticed, and share that with the class. If technology is readily available, have the group copy and paste selections from the essay into slides. Choose two speakers: one to summarize the article and its purpose, and the other to show how the writer used strategies they are learning. Final presentations should describe the article(s)' contents, kind(s) of writing, and special features the group has noticed. Remind students to include citations with the website name, title, authors, URL address, and the date they access the article.

Or you can organize a gallery walk for students to see and hear what their classmates have discovered. First, arrange students into groups numbered 1–5 based on their common essay. Group members discuss their essay and create a visual to augment their presentation: a poster, drawing on the whiteboard, or a set of simple electronic slides.

Then, set up four or five groups/stations—1–5. Next, have all the students number off 1–5. Those in the new group one, go to station one; new group two to station two, and so forth. Set timer for 2–3 minutes. Whoever in the group is standing in front of the poster their group prepared explains it succinctly to the group. Buzzer rings. Groups move to the right. Whoever in the group is in front of their own essay explains to the group. Continue until all have seen and explained the essays. See online videos for other ways to organize gallery walks.

The value of a gallery walk is twofold. The students are talking and making decisions about how to present what they are learning about published writing. You get to listen and observe with a smile. In an informal but efficient way, you have the opportunity to learn and plan based on what you hear and see.

A benefit of assigning students to bring in essay samples is the insight you gain into what interests your students. You can utilize that knowledge as you select topics for subsequent assignments. What makes this kind of student-generated assignment so rich is that students tend to read more when they get to choose what to contribute. Students usually want to make sure they understand the selection just in case you ask them to talk about it! In this case, you are.

DECIDE HOW LONG

So far, in earlier writing assignments, students have not been asked to argue a position to bring about a change in belief or behavior. They have, however, been gathering facts and writing about them in some logically organized fashion that will inspire interest and inform positions. Whatever the assignments though, students probably have begun to ask, "How long should this be?"

You may be tempted to say, "Long enough to get the job done," which is a good answer but not very helpful to inexperienced writers. Instead, you could go on to tell them that it should be complete. An essay, like a good story, should have at least three parts—a recognizable beginning, middle, and ending—and for an essay, the names of these parts are introduction, body, and conclusion.

Now would be a good time to review with your wondering writers the function of each of these parts of an essay. Yes, even if you have bright, experienced former honors' or AP students who have been writing very well all through high school, you must reinforce these functions in as much depth as needed for the students you currently are teaching and then hold them accountable for

- *introducing* their essays in ways that invite, intrigue, indicate the direction, and guide the reader into the body of the essay;

Figure 6.3   Train Couplings Signify Transitions. *iStock/lisafx.*

- *developing the middle* part of their essays with well-built paragraphs that include substantiated facts, opinions of experts, examples, and so on, sequenced in a logical order; and
- *concluding* their essays in a way that summarizes or reflects on what has been written (without repeating it), or projects into the future for consideration, all without introducing new information.

USE GRAPHICS TO SHOW STRUCTURE

Diagrams, cartoons, and other images can show the structure of an essay and the function of each part. Using such images enhances your instruction, making it easier for students to visualize different features of an effective essay. Consider using the idea of a train. It is a metaphor to illustrate both purpose and order that makes sense to students living in most geographical settings—city or country, mountain, or plains. Show the engine, the cargo cars, and the caboose. Students will get the message.

The engine is the introduction, gets the essay going, and pulls it along. The cargo cars are the body (whatever number is needed to carry the information). The caboose is the conclusion, signaling that the essay has come to an end. The couplings are the transitions (signal words) that both hold the ideas, words, sentences, and paragraphs together and show the relationships among those components. To see a sample of this train metaphor in slides, check the companion website for this book at www.planningwithpurpose.info.

WRITE ABOUT AND EXPLORE VISUALS

Just as travelers often visit art museums to learn more about a community, town, or culture, you can invite your students to view and write about art, pictures or photos as a way of learning and practicing argumentative writing. After doing an in-class activity described below, expand the experience out of class.

Begin with a common viewing experience, and then let students choose and write about their chosen photo or picture of art. The following activities are based on notes from a workshop "Entering Art" led by Terry and Jenny Williams at the Detroit Institute of Art.

Variations on the suggestions in the "Entering Art" assignments work to evoke inspiring student poetry as well as essays because art invites imaginative entry into its drama, mood, theme, locality, texture, and space. Both representational and abstract art can lure viewers into the artist's original act of creation. By all means, consider the cultural diversity in your class, college, or community. Consider, too, specifics images relating to your content area. Encourage students to connect what they see to topics you are teaching.

ENTER ART AND WRITE ABOUT IT

Art illuminates
we teach our students
and they understand.

—Anna Roseboro

This imaginative entry evokes all five senses, memories, and dreams as students look and allow themselves to feel and imagine. Allot a full 40 to 50 minutes for this assignment. Give students time for an experience that is personal and uniquely their own, time to put the experience into words that enrich both their own viewing and the work of art itself. And, so you can write along with your students, set the timer to ring 5 minutes before the end of the class meeting to have time to debrief.

1. Have a large, sharp copy of the artwork projected when the students arrive in the classroom.
2. Play soft, lyric-free instrumental music as a mood-creating background while students take their seats and you do that beginning of the period record-keeping.
3. Invite the students to join you, and all of you view the artwork silently for 3 minutes. Yes, three full minutes.
4. Then distribute the handout with the prompts you choose for the art you have. (Sample prompts follow in Figure 6.4.)
5. Read each step aloud slowly and softly, pausing between prompts to allow time for students to look at the art and respond mentally.

Finally, invite the students to choose the kind of "entry" they would like to write about, and let them write for the next 20 minutes or so. Join in the experience and write along with your students. See Figure 6.4 for prompts adapted from the museum notes.

> **TEXT BOX 6.4   ENTERING ART**
>
> 1. Step inside the artwork. Let its space become your space. What does it feel like as you journey into the painting? Where are you? What do you hear? Smell? What do you notice under your feet? Imagine you can touch something in the painting. What would that be? How would it feel?
> 2. Write about the artwork as if it were a dream. Bring the scene to life and leave us in that moment. Use "In a dream, I" or "Last night I had the strangest dream" or simply, "I dreamed."
> 3. Write about the scene as if it were happening now, using present tense and active verbs. Begin with "I am" Move around inside the work and make things happen. Begin a line with "Suddenly" in order to create surprise, moving into something unexpected.
> 4. Write about the work as if it were a memory. List short, separate memories or one long memory. Both invent and remember as you write.
> 5. Imagine the art as something you see outside a window. Begin with "From my window, I see."

Invite your students to turn to a partner and read what they have written. It is enlightening for students who have viewed the same picture to read aloud what they experienced.

You could extend this kind of exploring or writing and practice writing arguments based on art or photos. Direct your students to preselected website collections of art or photos like those on the Google Art Project or 24 Hours in Pictures. In the second instance, students could locate the photos taken on their own birth date. View all, choose one and write about it, paste a copy on their essay along with the URL of the site from which they found the photo, picture, or image.

The position statement or claim in their argument could be their explanation of why their chosen art, photo, or image is important or serendipitous for this particular class during this particular month of the year. The student's thesis statement would need to include an adjective or adverb which the body of the essay would substantiate. What does the student claim about the painting, photo, or image? Then, support that claim with an argument that compels the reader to give credence to the writer's choice. This assignment usually is both fun and insightful for both students and teachers. Moreover, students seldom realize until later, how much rhetorical preparation they are getting for writing academic essays that require substantiation of claims.

The multimodal component can easily be added by having a student copy and paste the image into their essay. They then must write a caption, a pithy description of the image, that includes something other than the title of the art or photo, and that links the image to their claim statement. Of course, students will include a citation of the source of the image they use.

SCHEDULE PEER-FEEDBACK IN-CLASS, THEN FOR HOMEWORK

Another version for designing lessons for students to read and comment on the writing of their peers follows here. In this case, students may comment in a class meeting or for homework. For the in-class version, as students arrive, have them sign up in one of the "color" groups. For homework, you could have the students pre-arranged in the five color-coded groups. In class or for homework, students can choose to respond to any three members in their assigned color group: red to blue, blue to green, green to orange, orange to purple, purple to yellow, and yellow to red. After you have modeled highlighting and inserting comments, students usually can handle this task with ease. Use the rubric you customized for this assignment, as suggested in chapter 1.

In the classroom or in virtual settings, based on the length of the writing and skill of your readers, set the timer for 10 to 12 minutes for students to read each paper. Review the rubric first; then instruct students to read and comment on something different on the writing by each of their three chosen classmates.

- Classmate A: CONTENT sufficient to meet requirements of assignment.
- Classmate B: STRUCTURE of essay, of paragraphs, of sentences.
- Classmate C: LANGUAGE, QUALITY OF RESOURCES or EVIDENCE, MUGS (mechanics, usage, grammar, spelling), and so on.

In this peer-feedback version, and in the one described later in chapter 7, students read three different drafts and receive feedback from three different readers. They see what works in the writing of their classmates and what does not; they may even notice ways to improve their own work. Using as a guide for commenting the same rubric or grading guidelines you will use to evaluate their writing reminds students of the assignment specifics and assessment guidelines.

Plan to have students "exercise" by giving courteous and useful feedback on short in-class writings you have assigned as free-writes or quick-writes at the beginning of class. Practice these strategies for giving and receiving feedback in class two or three times before assigning it for homework. The goal, in this case, is twofold: to show that first drafts need to be revised and that considerate, focused, constructive feedback from peers can be useful.

Figure 6.4 Encourage students to post questions of clarification. *iStock/fizkes.*

CONFERENCE TO CLARIFY STUDENT THINKING

No matter how well you have presented lessons or scheduled time for practice and review, sometimes only talking to individual students will ensure their learning. Begin right away modeling ways to respond to writing. Then have students work for short periods of time in pairs, reading and responding to each other's drafts, and then as small groups in structured R.A.G.s as described in chapter 2, or in the color-coded groups described in this chapter. Hold off scheduling one-on-one conferences until later in the course.

According to the CWPA Outcomes Statement goals and the goals of many college departments you are expected to design opportunities for students to,

- *Use composing processes and tools as a means to discover and reconsider ideas.*
- *Experience the collaborative and social aspects of writing processes.*
- *Learn to give and to act on productive feedback to works in progress.*[1]

It takes time for students to develop confidence in the peer-feedback experience and trust what they learn from reading the writing of others and taking seriously the comments of their classmates. But with time, they are less likely to depend solely on teacher feedback to decide what can be done to improve their own writing during the multiple revision steps and strategies they are learning.

Composing Compelling Arguments

Figure 6.5 **Have Students Come to Conferences with Written Questions.** *iStock/fizkes.*

PREP FOR ONE-ON-ONE CONFERENCES

How do you prepare students for conferencing so that they will bring some insight into their own reading or writing process and remain open to taking something valuable from the conversation? Have students come with specific written questions based on the assignment guidelines.

After they have (1) done in-class or observed online time for prewriting to prime the pumps, (2) written their first drafts to explore and organize their ideas, (3) used the grading rubric to read and revise, (4) participated in some form of peer-feedback task like the one described here or in the R.A.G. format described in chapter 2, and (5) have written a second revision they are ready to submit for grading, it will be soon enough to schedule the first one-on-one conferencing.

If you get involved too soon, students may think all they have to do is follow your advice and earn an A. You can avoid this expectation when you use the general grading guidelines for which an A is awarded for the student's own creative touch. Most can accomplish a C (complete—includes required components); you can teach a B (writing correctly with few distracting errors), and can only acknowledge the originality and creativity evident for the A. See the general grading guidelines discussion and diagram in chapter 1. In virtual settings, have students sign-up for appointments. Points may be deducted if the student misses the appointment without sending a note to reschedule.

WITHHOLD GRADES UNTIL ONE-ON-ONE CONFERENCES

Consider returning final written drafts with comments but withholding the grade until the students meet for the conference. Then they are more likely to pay attention to those time-consuming comments you write as you read and decide the grade. In this case, students could be advised to come to the conference with one section of the paper revised. You could start the conference asking the student, "Based on the comments on the essay I returned to you, what grade do you think you earned?" Then have students show you the revised section, discuss the merits of that revision, and answer questions students may have.

The grade on the original essay should not be changed unless it is clear you made an error. As you graded, you may have misread a passage. Upon meeting with the student and reading the section again, you see that you had docked points for something clearly written correctly. In that case, admit your error, modify the grade, and move on.

Encourage students to use what they learn during the conference when writing the next paper. Writing conferences themselves need not be graded, simply acknowledged with a check or plus in your grade book. (Check, they came; plus, they brought a revised section of the essay.)

Be aware that some college department policies require a certain number of one-on-one conferences with each student, each course. Course planners know that these meetings serve as a formative assessment for you and your students to learn more about ways they view their own writing and ways they approach revisions.

You will find that keeping some notes about these conferences provides good information for subsequent conferences and questions from supervising professors and department administrators, too. Having specific information about specific students demonstrates your attention to individuals that all value. Time, patience, modeling, adapting, and adjusting by both the students and teacher ultimately lead to productive one-on-one conferencing. By the end of the course, you may be able to report as Jessica Hudson, one of our GTA contributors wrote,

> A first-year composition class should give students many opportunities to try out different writing strategies, especially ones they might not have considered before, and revision can simply be another exercise in re-trying their essay (the French word for 'try') without the fear of failing.

TRAIN FOR SUCCESS

The first quarter at most college courses is much like preseason training for sports teams. It is not that the athletes do not know the rules or no longer have the physical prowess to play the game; the issue may be that the students probably have not had to utilize that knowledge or those muscles during the off-season. It is much the same with students and the reason teachers find themselves reviewing and reteaching what they know students have been taught before, not because the students do not know but because they have not been using what they had learned.

You know about that yourself. When you are preparing to teach a lesson, you are reviewing details about general topics you know you have known for years. What's that adage? If they don't use it, they'll lose it. Therefore, go ahead and reteach and then begin again to hold the students accountable for using what they are learning again.

RELEASE SOME CONTROL TO STUDENT STARTERS

About a third of the way through the course is a good time to gradually release some of the control of the class. Let the students do more while you observe and adjust your lessons based on what you notice. One efficient way to do this is to offer students the option to earn extra credit by being a student starter. This just means on the approved day, based on a calendar you provide, a student starts the class with a 5–7-minute presentation!

Plan ahead by setting up a calendar on which students can add their names but not make changes to the document. Choose days when students are not scheduled to make oral presentations. (See schedule for that in chapter 8.) Student starters earn full credit for making on-topic, on-time presentations; these presentations do not create extra work for you once you set up the calendar.

MOST ARE INTERESTED IN THE 5Ws
AND H FOR STUDENT STARTERS

- Who? You.
- What? Whatever seems appropriate to you that shows some connection to what we've studied in the past couple of weeks. See HOW?
- When? On the date you've signed up to speak during the first 5–7 minutes of class.
- Where? Here in our classroom.
- Why? Because what you have to say can help us learn. This is a way for you to practice your presentation skills and earn full credit for an on-time, within time, and appropriate presentation.

- How? Your choice of what's appropriate. Could be a dramatic reading from the text; a poem, song, or video clip (previewed by the instructor)
  - relates to, explains, explores, and expands the topic we're studying;
  - makes a relevant connection to something studied in another course;
  - is something experienced, observed, or viewed on TV or online and links to our course.

Most instructors are pleasantly surprised at how effective this option is for support of their teaching and evidence of student learning.

CONCLUSION

As they explore with their peers, paying attention to features in the different texts, the emerging writers begin using this knowledge in their own reading and their own writing. By this time, your student traveling companions are prepared for the more sophisticated thinking required to write convincing arguments and persuasive essays and speeches, as described in chapter 7, "Writing Persuasively to Impact Thinking and Behavior," and chapter 8, "Writing for Speaking and Multimodal Presentations." Some students will feel competent and confident about composing arguments so compelling that their writing and speaking inspires serious consideration of controversial issues. The oral and multimodal presentations your students present may even bring about changes in the beliefs and behaviors of their audiences and viewers. To prepare for online presentations, review with students the learning platform you will use. Will there be a live audience? Will students create and save an mp4 video that classmates will view in live synchronous or asynchronous setting?

NOTE

1. Council of Writing Program Administrators, "WPA Outcomes Statement for First-Year Composition (3.0)."

Chapter 7

Writing Persuasively to Impact Thinking and Behavior

If you would persuade, you must appeal to interest rather than intellect[1]

—Benjamin Franklin

Effective writers and speakers are those who identify specific values held by members of their audience and then compose communication to appeal to their heads, their hearts, and their pockets. Convincing writing presents sound reasons that motivates a specific audience and shows how a proposed change in attitude or behavior can benefit the individuals in that audience. Therefore, it is critical to discern, ahead of time, what members in the target audience think is important and then construct arguments that appeal to that.

Respected writers and orators are those who can be trusted to act with integrity. They resist the temptation to twist evidence and to use sloppy, fallacious reasoning. It is the kind of honesty you strive to instill in your students. This chapter can help guide your lesson planning to reinforce critical thinking and inspire students to learn the importance of implementing credible compositions with skillful sensitivity. This will be a key skill for students who follow a career for which they must seek grants to fund their work.

Start the series of lessons by introducing and reviewing ways to locate and evaluate resources and select appropriate facts, opinions, and reasons students can use to substantiate their claims. Doing so leads to outcome goals of your course like those in the Council of Writing Program Administrators (CWPA), which states: "Critical thinking is the ability to analyze, synthesize, interpret, and evaluate ideas, information, situations, and texts."[2] Continue with lessons that model written and visual media, then assign students to compose their own persuasive presentations incorporating evidence and compelling arguments. Analyzing written and visual texts to discover probable attitudes and values of an audience can enhance students' ability to read more critically and write more carefully.

As they prepare to write their persuasive essays, students must identify the purpose and audience for their own paper, product (slides, video, podcast), or presentation. Students can start by considering the terms in the list below, then asking the question: "What do I want my audience to know, believe, and do once they read, hear, or view what I have composed?"

Share the explanations that follow:

- *Beliefs*—what is accepted as fact—"The temperature is below freezing." "The Great Spirit created the universe."
- *Attitude*—what is believed about forces outside one's control that makes the proposed change favorable/unfavorable, safe/unsafe, legal/illegal, or positive/negative based on the audience's beliefs. "My boss will never give me a ____." "I'll be fired if I go." "That group never liked me anyway."
- *Values*—the principles on which one bases their lives: moral codes, beliefs about what is right or wrong (often related to religion and/or politics). "It is dishonest to steal, even when you're hungry." "Our family always votes."

Ask students to return to a model text you already assigned. Have them mark passages showing what the writers reveal about the beliefs, attitudes, and values of their audiences. Then identify the kinds of arguments the writer offers to suggest that a change in belief or behavior would be a good or right thing to do. In what ways do proposed changes benefit the members of the audience, a group of people, or issues the audience cares about?

Have students identify the writers' tone—attitude toward the topic of articles and essays—by paying attention to words, phrases, and imagery the writers use to make their point. Soon your most skeptical students discover each writer's audience and purpose.

The CWPA Outcomes Statement says that students should be able to "recognize and evaluate underlying assumptions, read across texts for connections and patterns, identify and evaluate chains of reasoning."[3] These close readings reveal attitudes, and behavior writers use directly or indirectly to invite or attempt to persuade readers to adopt. As you select material for writing assignments, also consider mentor texts that students can model as they write about topics that interest them. Ask students to put arguments on a scale to see how effective they are to the audience the students have identified. The insight gained from such exercises inspires students to utilize what they are learning as they compose their own work.

Figure 7.1   What Arguments Tip the Scales in Favor of Writer's Claim? *iStock/bagrovskam.*

DISCOVER WAYS THAT COMPELLING ARGUMENTS PRECEDE PERSUADING

Writers need to know something about their reader/audience to choose convincing facts and use compelling reasons that will be persuasive. One effective way to illustrate this fact is to have students draft a letter to persuade their parents or employer to permit them to do something heretofore forbidden. Students understand they must come up with both facts and reasons to get permission to do that forbidden thing and must not finagle with facts or use faulty reasoning.

Once students have giggled and guffawed about times they have gotten caught doing either of these things, present a lesson on the ethics of argumentation. Keep it light, but keep it real, even share a story of your own. Consider conducting a few rounds of S.P.A.R.s, as described in chapter 6. Ask students to pay special attention to rebuttals. Are they on target? The value of S.P.A.R. ring is that students hear how important it is to counter opposing views without insulting the intelligence of the reader/audience. If the writer/speaker does not appear to accept that the other side has valid reasons for holding to those beliefs or behaviors, the reader/audience is likely to close down and stop reading or listening.

UNVEIL ARISTOTLE'S ART OF RHETORIC

Then take the students back a couple millennia and embellish your mini-lesson with the classical foundation of the art of rhetoric—honesty in arguing—as attributed to Aristotle. You may find cartoons that will keep it simple, while telling the story that, for eons, an essential part of a classical education has been learning to argue well. Your students readily accept that writers and speakers who can convince the audience to change are those who rise to become leaders. Invite students to name influential leaders they know about from history, movies, and current events.

Go ahead and use the Greek words "ethos," "pathos," and "logos." These are premium root words for students to know because they make up much of the academic vocabulary college students encounter. No need to belabor the points or require students to memorize definitions of each Greek term. The purpose is to show that what they are studying now has been a part of education curricula for centuries.

VIEW SAMPLES TO ENHANCE UNDERSTANDING ABOUT FALLACIES

Mallory Jones, one of our graduate teaching assistant contributors, wrote:

> I decided to search YouTube for videos that I could show to help explain rhetoric to them better than I could. I found a Ted Talk called *"How to Use Rhetoric to Get What You Want,"* and the speaker was Camille A. Langston. . . . The videos helped my students understand what rhetoric is, so I started to incorporate commercials to analyze how the advertisers used rhetoric. After doing this exercise, my students were confident moving forward with their persuasive essays.

You can have comparable success with your students. Before sending students off to write their persuasive essays and speeches, bring in print, media, and digital advertisements to show how even the most astute among us are persuaded to buy clothes, food, games, or sugary drinks. Viewing commercials that manipulate prospective customers helps students develop an understanding about ethos, pathos, and logos more quickly than simply hearing the terms defined.

As noted in the CWPA Outcomes Statement, "When writers think critically about the materials they use—whether print texts, photographs, data sets, videos, or other materials—they separate assertion from evidence . . . and compose appropriately qualified and developed claims and generalizations."[4] After showing examples of your own, invite students to search for examples on their tablets or phones.

If time permits, present a lesson about fallacies that includes bandwagoning, hasty generalization, snob appeal, slippery slope, and appeal to authority. Most of your students will be able to recognize these fallacies in advertisements they see online, on television, and in magazines; they just may not know the proper descriptive terms. Teaching them about fallacies in advertisements helps students become not only more critical consumers of media but also more conscientious composers of communique. Students will be more alert as they choose the images and visual aids for their oral and multimodal presentations.

You could use the grading rubric in figure 7.2 to have students return to some of the selected videos and, in pairs or small groups, critique those videos. You may customize elements in the rubric in figure 7.2 to create the grading guidelines for the multimodal presentations you assign later.

Rubric for MULTIMODAL PRESENTATIONS

INTRODUCTION

Exemplary - 5	Proficient - 3	Incomplete - 1
Unique and memorable introduction engages audience immediately and communicates with words and images purpose of the presentation.	Introduces topic and purpose in an engaging manner.	Introduction is not included or does not make sense. Topic and purpose are not clear.

CONTENT

Exemplary - 5	Proficient - 3	Incomplete - 1
Creativity, cited evidence, and chosen images blend in an innovative way, the purpose of the presentation for specified audience.	Creative elements are included, but evidence and explanations do little to enhance presentation for the specified audience or purpose	No creative elements are included, or the types of evidence and explanations are inappropriate or distract from the content and/or purpose of the presentation for the specified audience.
The specified audience would learn something from the presentation and find it valuable.	The presentation is appropriate for the specified audience.	The content and language of the piece is not appropriate for the specified audience.

IMAGES/GRAPHICS

Exemplary - 5	Proficient - 3	Incomplete - 1
The graphics and images contribute to a creative and effective presentation and enhance key points by contributing to the concept explanation.	The graphics relate to the spoken words and help communicate the content.	The graphics distract from the explanations or don't relate to the spoken words and made in this presentation.

TECHNICAL PRODUCTION

Exemplary - 5	Proficient - 3	Incomplete - 1
Smooth transitions throughout piece. No dead space.	Transitions are smooth, but dead space is occasionally heard.	Much of the piece has distracting background noise. Transitions are jumpy.
Audio volume complements the presentation.	Volume is acceptable.	Volume changes are highly distracting.
Length of the media piece was appropriate.	Piece would benefit by being more concise or including more explanation.	Piece doesn't follow teacher guidelines for media length of the media.

DELIVERY

Exemplary - 5	Proficient -3	Incomplete -1
Presenter sounds comfortable with the content. Words are clear and pacing is appropriate for the specified audience.	Presenter has fairly smooth delivery. Words are clear; pacing for chosen specified audience is appropriate	Delivery interferes with ability to understand or follow the piece. Words often aren't clear and pacing is irregular.
Correct grammar is used consistently or is adjusted for specified audience.	Grammatical and pronunciation mistakes are few.	Grammatical mistakes and mispronunctiation interfere with ability to understand the piece.

Figure 7.2 Use Rubric for Critiquing Visual Media. *Created by author.*

ALLOW STUDENTS TO CHOOSE ISSUES THAT MATTER

Reading maketh a full man, conference a ready man, and writing an exact man[5]

—Sir Francis Bacon

Students are more enticed to learn when they see an immediate purpose. Jessica Hudson, one of our graduate teaching assistant contributors, noted in her reflection that when her students can't justify the assignment, "the writing process becomes a battlefield . . . Writing anything, even prewriting sometimes, can be a stressful or at least unwelcome endeavor." Lesson ideas that follow can help you prepare for your battlefield.

An appealing reason for students to use their newly crafted skills is to conduct research and compose essays or speeches to persuade a specific audience to change a policy or a law about something important to the students. They can use the same strategies in academic papers designed for their chosen audience as they did to write letters to their parents or employers.

If they have no passion for a topic, students may invest less effort into planning and composing compelling essays using credible evidence from research that answer these kinds of questions,

- What is the problem?
- What does the audience believe or feel about the problem? How do you know?
- What has the audience said or done to show that is what they believe or feel?
- What should be done to try to solve the problem? How do you know?
- Which arguments will appeal to the head (facts), the heart (emotions), and the pocket (financial cost)?
- Why will a change in belief or action benefit the audience?
- How will life be better once the change is in place?

Now that they have a better understanding of

- knowing their audience,
- marshaling their facts,
- articulating reasons for change, and
- practicing countering arguments,

students are ready to write more nuanced essays. They can focus on a specific purpose that will compel readers to take notice and maybe even take action and become part of the solution.

DEMONSTRATE CAREFUL STEPS TO EFFECTIVE WRITING

Don't get it right.
Get it written,
Then get it right.[6]

—Goran "George" Moberg

Students sometimes wonder how they can make a well-written early draft even better. If you encourage students to write about what's important to them, reiterate that writing is a process, and teach specific steps to take to improve their writing, you will have taught them a life skill. Here's a scaffolding approach using alliterative terms, the "Five Es for Revision."

During revision, encourage students to do the following:

- *Expand*: develop what is written to make ideas clearer and more interesting without being repetitive. Add more information to show rather than tell. Use carefully chosen examples from literature (any reading and viewing), life (personal experiences and observations), and lessons learned in other courses.
- *Explain*: clarify what is written by using various reasons based on experiences, observations, and lessons learned in other courses. Pull ideas together with reasons.
- *Exchange and rearrange*: determine what words can be substituted to make the writing clearer, more interesting, and more precise. Substitute abstract nouns with concrete nouns; create words in light of the positive or negative connotations that evoke the mood (emotion) you want the audience to experience. In what ways can words, sentences, and paragraphs be rearranged to make ideas unfold more smoothly and the writer's thoughts clearer, more interesting, and inviting?
- *Expunge*: get rid of distracting or weak words, phrases, and sentences that cloud communication. They prevent ideas from glowing with authority as they inform, convince, persuade, and even entertain.
- *Enliven*: consider using more active verbs instead of passive ones in forms of the verb "to be."

USE CRITERIA TO MEASURE RESPONSES TO READING AND VIEWING

New college students sometimes wonder why their instructors get so excited about literature and media that may not interest their students. Each reader has individual standards measuring what is interesting and worthwhile. Share a set of criteria for evaluating texts and media, which establishes a prelude for writing thoughtful evaluations of various modes and genres. Rating what they read or view can demonstrate that they are reaching standards measuring their ability to make thoughtful assessments of print, digital, and film media, and eventually write stronger critiques.

Working as a class, ask students to score their response to a text or video they already have studied together. Try to mask your own opinions as students add their comments as they talk about the following:

- CLARITY: how easy or difficult the text or media was to understand when they read or viewed.
- ESCAPE: how much they found themselves drawn away from their everyday life as they read the text or viewed the media.
- REFLECTION OF REAL LIFE: how much the people and places seemed familiar or reflect life as the student knows it.
- ARTISTRY IN DETAILS: Did the student find the selection engaging enough to reread/review? Did the author use fresh imagery, realistic dialogue, or sparkling vocabulary that made the reader pause, bask in the beauty of the passage or scene? Similar criteria may be applied to a director's use of camera angles and shots, lighting, and music.
- INTERNAL CONSISTENCY: if the text or video flows well and all parts seem to fit in a meaningful way, some students will give the work high marks. On the other hand, if either seems disjointed or has scenes that could be deleted without being missed, some will give the piece low marks.
- TONE: readers/viewers tend to respond positively or negatively to something read or viewed because they appreciate how well an author's tone, personal style, or attitude comes through the composition. They know what to expect and look forward to experiencing the work that clearly reveals what elicited such feelings. Some may rate high the selection that creates a strong emotional response, whether it is a positive or negative one. The moods created may be lasting and universal.
- PERSONAL BELIEFS: in another vein, writing may be appealing to certain readers/viewers simply because it confirms their personal beliefs. Even if readers cannot articulate their reactions, all are influenced by their own ideas relating to religion, politics, social issues—attitudes about what is moral or immoral, right or wrong.
- SIGNIFICANT INSIGHT: perhaps the quality of the composition that is more difficult to convey relates to its ability to provide a window and mirror to life, offering new insight into individuals, groups, places, and situations. The text may compel those who experience it to consider their own behaviors and thoughts about life and death, good and evil. This is especially

challenging as college students begin to experience more culturally diverse texts than they may have encountered earlier. But, don't let that stop you from offering students the opportunity to evaluate print and media texts using these nine yardsticks of value. Consider using one of the tech apps, like TwitterChat, that invites viewers to post their opinions anonymously where the whole class can view the responses at once.

CHART RESPONSES TO GATHER DATA FOR WRITING

You and your students can use these nine lenses to organize your thoughts on the value of what you read and view. Ask them to rate each criterion on a scale value of 1–5 (low to high). (See figure 7.3.)

As students record responses, remind them to include in their notes specific references to the text or media. They will need those examples to flesh out their evaluative review in discussion and/or writing. During the mini-lesson about the common text, invite students to quote a short phrase or sentence; suggest keywords as examples; and identify page numbers, paragraph numbers, or reference to specific scenes. Take time to point out online tools for citing such references using the citation style of your college.

Nine YARDSTICKS of Value

Yardstick	1	2	3	4	5
Clarity					
Escape					
Reflection					
Artistry					
Internal Consistency					
Tone					
Emotional					
Personal					
Significance					

Figure 7.3 Chart Text Evaluation as a Prewriting Strategy. *Walter Blair and John Gerber, eds.,* Better Reading Two: Literature, *3rd ed.*

ORGANIZE NOTES TO WRITE INSIGHTFUL CRITIQUES

Once they have their prewriting notes, students are ready to think about how to pull them all together into a well-structured piece of argumentative writing that explains why they evaluated the experience as they have. Questions to consider are the following:

- What is your *general response* to this selection? Strong, moderate, weak?
- Why have you *ranked* the work as you have?
- What specific references from the selection can you *cite to explain and support* your opinion? Which quotations or references will best show what you want to say?

Next, students decide the best way to organize their thoughts. They could write about

- strong qualities to weak—those they rate highest to those that rate lowest;
- more personal qualities to less personal ones;
- vice versa, or
- some other way.

Remind students to include in the opening paragraph the title and author of the work as well as their general response to it. This will be an opinion word, an adjective, or adverb that will guide their writing and alert their reader about what will follow. The evaluation may begin with a carefully selected quotation that reflects the strong point the student writer will explore and expand in the remainder of the critique.

Together, once you introduce this way of looking at text and media, look at reviews found on websites that sell books or videos. These models are a good start for your students. Many published reviewers and film critics reflect, directly or indirectly, each of the criteria you are asking your students to consider. Consider adapting the criteria for your specific content area.

After creating a chart of their responses and looking at sample critiques, your students should be ready to compose their own essays or videos. These can provide written evidence of their ability to write a fully developed composition that persuasively shows their careful consideration of many aspects of a published work they have read or video they have viewed.

This evaluative writing may be adapted to reflections in students' majors or fields of study. The students could apply similar evaluations to print and digital presentations about science, medicine, or engineering; consider new technology, an historical document they are using in another course, or something written about a current event. You know your students, what you are teaching, and what learning you need to measure. Adapt as needed to achieve your own course outcome goals.

DECIDE AND WRITE FOR A SPECIFIC AUDIENCE

For the major paper on writing an essay to persuade the audience to change its belief or behavior, invite students to choose a topic on something that interests them personally or one they are studying in another course. This will reinforce or expand their thinking about that topic and earn them credit for completing an assignment in your class.

This is an opportune time to remind students about their audience and the kind of language they can use effectively to express their ideas. For example, if they choose to argue about reducing injuries in a particular sport and are speaking to sports fans, the writer is right to use sports-specific jargon and slang.

To demonstrate this fact, ask your students what this sentence means: "The difficulty of your set could be increased if you do a jam followed by a peach." Class members familiar with gymnastics will understand the speaker is describing the point value of a gymnastics routine. The sentence means that the point values you can earn on your gymnastics routine can be bigger if you include, in sequence, two particular skills on the uneven parallel bars: the "jam," which leaves the gymnast sitting on the high bar; and the "peach," where the gymnast moves from the high bar to the low bar.

If, on the other hand, the essay is being written to be delivered at a school board meeting made up of neighbors from many walks of life, the writer would choose a more general language. This will likely be understood by an audience less familiar with the lingo of the sport and include explanations when that lingo is spoken.

The same care in choosing language would be true if the student is writing about dance, music, or art, or to an audience familiar with a specific culture or event. In each case, the prior knowledge of the audience with the topic should determine the language the writer chooses in the final text version of the essay, article, letter, or media presentation. So, include in plans for writing the requirement that students identify their target audience. They should show what the writers believe their named audience knows and believes about the topic of the essay or presentation. Such specific information can guide the students as they conduct research and select supportive evidence and compelling rationales that explain, explore, and clarify the claims the students make in the essay.

90 Chapter 7

WRITE FROM RESEARCH: A SUMMATIVE ASSESSMENT

Having students write argumentative and persuasive essays is an appropriate assignment to explore resources available through research. During the second half of the course, design some mini-lessons that point out a range of reference materials that published writers use. Consider how often one sees definitions, quotations, anecdotes, personal experiences, and references to current events in editorials and speeches.

College students are familiar with dictionaries, newspapers, and magazines but may not know about collections of quotations and anecdotes. Students usually know they must acknowledge sources from which they borrow and use information but may not have had many assignments asking them to show they know how to do so.

Consider a short writing assignment that requires them to use a variety of reference materials. They could write an editorial on an abstract term and then present their ideas in a short informal speech as it relates to the content area they are learning with you. The CWPA Outcomes Statement says students should "Explore the concepts of intellectual property (such as fair use and copyright) that motivate documentation conventions" and "Practice applying citation conventions systematically in their own work."[7] A short assignment can help meet both these outcomes.

WRITE ABOUT AN ABSTRACT TERM

For this writing-speaking assignment, students can draw from a hat an abstract term like those in figure 7.4. Then from specified resources, gather information to write an editorial that can be converted into a short

apathy	irritation	satisfaction
beauty	loneliness	simplicity
conceit	misery	surprise
cowardice	optimism	suspicion
dignity	patience	sympathy
elegance	pleasure	trust
failure	regret	worry

Figure 7.4   Use Abstract Terms for Practicing Basic Research. *Created by author.*

persuasive speech designed to raise the awareness of readers and listeners about their chosen term. The editorial and speech should give significant reasons to strive to achieve or to avoid an experience with that abstract idea like those in the list.

Roz Roseboro, one of our graduate teaching assistant contributors, assigns students to link the abstract term to the topic they have selected for their persuasive essay. This is another efficient way to have students explore and expand their thinking about that chosen topic before they write their major paper.

Adjust the list to meet the language skills of your students. More than one student can have the same term, which makes for interesting reading, seeing how different students handle the same word. Or have students work in pairs, and add a visual component where students include a collage or a set of five to six slides to supplement their oral presentation. Search "ReadWriteThink PDF" and find "Creating a PowerPoint Slide" and "PowerPoint Tool Tips" for further instructions.

The primary goals of the abstract term assignment are to learn about and use a variety of resources in persuasive writing. The final presentation on the abstract term should include five of the following six kinds of support:

- Definition of chosen term.
- Quotation using the term.
- Anecdote—could be an example from texts read together in class.
- Some sort of statistic or number relating to their term that supports their claim(s).
- Personal experience or observation of the term in action.
- Contemporary issue or situation illustrating the term.

Students will be expected to cite their sources, so this assignment can be a fine summative assessment of a variety of skills you are required to teach. You should know which citation style is used in your college or department—Chicago, MLA, APA, or another. Students will be held accountable for using citations correctly as they continue their academic study at the college and in much of the writing they do in the future.

REVIEW AND INTRODUCE REFERENCE RESOURCE MATERIALS

To assure that students are prepared for this complex assignment, consider a series of mini-lessons reviewing ways to find and use various kinds of resources. Your students may have had experiences with some reference materials but may have forgotten a few finer points. You should be able to locate several websites with lessons to help you plan appropriately for your students. Some sites even have quizzes to test student understanding before you move to the next reference resource. Consider making these nongraded activities as games for pairs using online quiz games played on tablets.

Confirming what students know avoids the desperate situations several of our GTA contributors mentioned in their reflections. Telling is not the same as teaching. They assumed their students knew or would know once told. These new instructors are now committing to including time for in-class practice for students to refresh and tone up those mental muscles.

If your students do not have consistent access to online resources, allot in-class time for students to search for just the right quotation. This is another way of assuring they understand how to search and navigate online, and how to cite what they find. From the collection of quotations, students should find one that includes their abstract term. A well-chosen quotation can illustrate or drive home the point the students want to make about their specific term.

Allotting in-class time to work under your tutelage will save you time when papers are turned in for grading. The goal here is to determine what students know before sending them off to work independently.

Figure 7.5 Teach with Games to Energize Thinking and Assess Learning. *iStock/monkeybusinessimages.*

USE STORIES AND STATISTICS TO APPEAL TO THE HEART AND THE HEAD

After explaining to your students that anecdotes are usually short narrations of an interesting, amusing, or biographical incident, share a couple of your favorites. They should be brief enough to be told in sixty to seventy-five seconds and chosen to appeal to the heart to be convincing. Show your listeners how these little stories can further explain or demonstrate the writer's or speaker's point. Encourage them to listen for similar stories in other settings—classes, political events, worship settings.

If your students are recent English language learners, it may be useful to find an anecdote translated from their native language. Many students will recognize this storytelling as a familiar strategy for clarifying and confirming a point. A lesson on anecdotes is a culturally responsive way to invite students to share teaching stories their families tell.

Statistics may be a challenge for students to find. But because many readers and listeners are impressed by numbers, using statistics ethically can be a

Compelling Arguments

Appeal to head...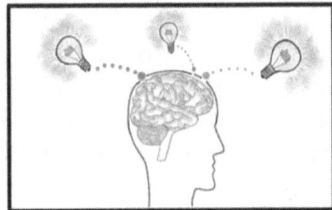

...heart...

...and pocket.

Figure 7.6 Compelling Arguments Appeal to Head, Heart, and Pocket. *Created by author.*

powerful, persuasive strategy that appeals to the head and the heart. Students are familiar with statistics in sports, movies, and music, and on commercials that relate percentages about the number of people who use or are impacted by certain products or services. How are statistics used in your content area?

People young and old are enticed to do or buy something if it puts them in the popular majority group. Advertisers frequently use bandwagoning—the suggestion that everyone is doing it. It can be a persuasive appeal that uses specific numbers. From their studies in science and social studies, students already may be familiar with the use of numbers to make a point in terms of ecology and demographics. Invite students to use numbers from one of those commercials or classes if they will work in their article, essay, or speech.

CONNECT TOPICS TO CURRENT EVENTS

Requiring that student writing and oral presentations include evidence based on a contemporary issue or situation is a good reason to teach students how to read and extrapolate information from print or digital news articles. Your writers should pay attention to current events and choose one that illustrates a reason to strive for or avoid an experience with their abstract term. Remind them to record when and where they get their facts.

It is important to teach students the basics of citing resources as a matter of academic honesty. Whatever they borrow should be acknowledged. For less experienced students, on earlier assignments, you may simplify the task by requiring only a list of resources consulted—an alphabetized list of the websites, books, and articles from which students borrow information for use in their writing or speaking.

The minimum list of resources for an early assignment may include (1) a dictionary, and sources for (2) quotations, (3) anecdotes, (4) statistics, (5) opinion of expert(s), and (6) current events. Remind students to alphabetize the list by author or title. For some, this alphabetized list will be a first step to creating official bibliographies or lists of sources consulted.

By the end of the course, all students should be required to show they know how to write endnotes. Because of the in-class demonstrations, time to verify during peer-editing sessions, students develop confidence and competence to handle this academic task. They should be able to explain when, where, why, and how they include references in their writing. (See chapter 4 "Writing to Clarify Thinking," for prompts that elicit written explanations of what students are learning.) They should also show how a number in the text links to an endnote that indicates what has been borrowed from a specific article or book. That resource must then be listed in the bibliography according to the citation style used at your college or in the student's particular area of study: humanities or sciences.

Extend your teaching by posting on your class website links to sites with samples and tutorials for creating citations. Posting on your website is worthwhile because (1) students have access when they need it, (2) they will not have to keep asking you, using valuable class time. Include checking citations for the correct format as an in-class peer-editing task. Also, since citations will be checked during peer-editing steps, (3) your grading will take less time because more assignments will be cited correctly.

ORGANIZE THE RESEARCHED INFORMATION

Once you have introduced and reviewed the variety of available resources and given students time to practice using them, give the abstract term or persuasive writing assignment. Here are some guidelines to help students organize their writing.

INTRODUCTION

- Dramatic opening that links to the idea of the essay/speech—could begin with an anecdote, quotation, or startling statistic.
- Transition to signpost—two or three sentences that link opening ideas to their purpose/thesis/claim statement.
- Purpose/thesis/claim, signpost statement—shows writer/speaker will follow a specific organizational pattern in the body of essay/speech
  - chronology: in order of time,
  - cause and effect: tell about a problem and the effect of it,
  - order of importance: most important idea to least or the opposite,
  - problem/solution: describe a problem and offer a solution.

BODY

- Incorporate five of the six kinds of evidence listed earlier.
- Appropriate transitions (refer to a list of transitions/signal words).
- Anything else the writer/speaker thinks will make the essay/speech more interesting to read or hear.

CONCLUSION

- Memorable closing: could save quotation for closing.
- Summary of key ideas.

- Challenge to attain or avoid experience with the idea of the abstract term.
- Call for change: urging reader/listener to strive to attain or avoid experience with the term Students should be encouraged to draft their essay/speech using these guidelines but be free to adjust them during revision stages.

ALLOT TIME TO GIVE AND PROCESS PEER FEEDBACK

Another version of designing lessons for students to read and comment on the writing of their peers follows here. Students may comment in class or for homework. Have five color-coded groups, and students can choose to respond to any three members in their assigned group: red to blue, blue to green, green to orange, orange to purple, purple to yellow, and yellow to red.

In this version of giving and receiving feedback from peers you may decide to use a version of the basic or customized Six Traits Writing rubric and organize responses based on those. This time students respond as follows:

- Classmate A: comment on traits 1 and 4 (CONTENT and WORD CHOICE).
- Classmate B: comment on traits 2 and 5 (ORGANIZATION and SENTENCE FLUENCY).
- Classmate C: comment on traits 3 and 6 (VOICE and CONVENTIONS).

Then, have students open and read comments on their own papers, write a three-step plan for revision (I will improve content, organization, language, etc. by ____), and send plans to you by email, if students are working online. If handwritten, they should show the plan to you before the class ends.

In this peer feedback format students read three different drafts and receive feedback from three different readers. Before assigning peer feedback as a homework assignment, spend a little time in class reviewing the process. After doing each task in class a couple of times, students usually handle this well outside of class. Consider using Flip-Grid or other audio recording applications for students to give and receive feedback, too.

Roz Roseboro pairs students who read and comment on each other's drafts for homework. They bring those comments and meet with their partner during class. Each can assume the persona of their partner's stated audience. The face-to-face conversation reinforces the CWPA outcome goals of collaboration and understanding of one's audience.

Many students look forward to the opportunity to give and receive feedback before they revise again. You can observe in class and view their comments online; you may record credit for participating in this writing process step, and see what issues need to be addressed in the next class meeting. Allotting

Figure 7.7 Why Should the Audience Care about the Chosen Topic? *iStock/ MachineHeadz.*

time for peer feedback and revision is worthwhile. Better writing accrues, and you can spend less time grading and writing responses.

CONCLUSION

It may take several weeks to make the trip from reviewing expository/informative writing to teaching argumentative and persuasive writing. However, if you know where you are heading, the expedition does not seem interminable if you are confident that you have not gotten lost.

Stop occasionally to rest and enjoy the side trips that confirm the value of teaching different modes of writing. Look at ways published writers and speakers in your content areas use the traits you are teaching. Invite students to bring in examples they see in other classes, in their own independent reading, in media they experience, or even point them out in texts you have read together in class. Craft lessons for students to model what they read and view.

By the final weeks of the course, on the last few miles of the journey, your students will be more confident and competent persuasive communicators. They understand the purpose of different kinds of writing and appreciate the ethics of argumentation, value of organization, and importance of respecting their reader/audience. Equally important, your students will have become more critical readers and listeners, more alert to ways others may use these skills to convince readers/listeners/viewers to change their beliefs and behavior.

The closing chapter of this book describes methods, materials, and management strategies for incorporating multimodal components in various compositions and genres of communication.

NOTES

1. Benjamin Franklin, *Quotes.net*, accessed April 2, 2020, https://www.quotes.net/quote/3919.

2. Council of Writing Program Administrators, "WPA Outcomes Statement for First-Year Composition (3.0)."

3. Ibid.

4. Francis Bacon, Forbes Quotes, accessed April 2, 2020, https://www.forbes.com/quotes/2933/.

5. Goran "George" Moberg, *Writing in Groups: New Techniques for Good Writing without Drills*, 3rd ed. (New York: The Writing Consultant, 1984).

6. Council of Writing Program Administrators, "WPA Outcomes Statement for First-Year Composition (3.0)."

Chapter 8

Writing for Speaking and Multimodal Presentations

The mark of an effective speaker is the ability to adapt to a variety of audiences and settings and to perform appropriately in diverse social situations.[1]

—Clella Jaffe

Composing successful communication requires careful consideration of one's purpose and audience, and also deciding which multimodal components can augment the written or oral presentation. A Kettering College Writing Center document reminds college teachers that "many students will have to present information in their careers or future classes that will require them to move beyond alphabetic text."[2] In this closing chapter of PLANNING WITH PURPOSE, we describe classroom-proven strategies for designing effective multimodal projects.

In its section on rhetorical knowledge, the Council of Writing Program Administrators (CWPA) Outcomes Statement notes that students should "Gain experience reading and composing in several genres to understand how genre conventions are shaped by readers' and writers' practices and purposes."[3] Students also should "understand and use a variety of technologies to address a range of audiences."[4] Sample assignments that follow call for students to analyze and critique live and recorded presentations. These assignments prepare students to incorporate appropriate gestures, posters, and props. Students can use electronic applications like PowerPoint, Keynote, or Prezzi to enhance the delivery of the oral presentations you assign.

NOTE WHAT MAKES AN EFFECTIVE ORAL PRESENTATION

Start this study on oral presentations querying students about what they notice about a good speaker. Surprisingly, they seldom comment on the contents of the speech. Instead, they point out aspects of delivery, like giving verbal clues to organization patterns, making eye contact, using gestures, rate of speaking, clear articulation, varied intonation, and poise. Your students may not use these terms, but what they do identify shows clearly that *how* the report is delivered is the key feature that makes the speech an effective form of communicating.

To guide your students to becoming more effective, capable, and self-assured speakers, incorporate into your lesson plans opportunities for students to observe and critique good speaking, as well as time to write, practice, and make their own presentations. If you integrate listening and giving courteous, constructive feedback to presentations, you all win. Students will be practicing critical listening skills, and you will have less out-of-class grading to complete alone.

Watch television news reporters. Show short video clips of politicians, sports figures, and businesspeople giving oral and media presentations. Include inspirational or motivational speakers. Bring in samples of podcasts, YouTube videos, and other modes of oral presentation with which students may be familiar. Just search the Internet for TedTalks Ed for brief versions to show and analyze in class.

Urge your students to observe their instructors. Ask students to reflect on the delivery styles of their clergy. Very soon, your learners can assemble a list of those characteristics of content, structure, style, and vocal qualities that make oral speeches simple to follow and easy to remember.

Students soon realize that giving an oral presentation is more than reading an essay aloud. Speaking is both an oral and visual presentation designed for a specific audience, place, and purpose. On close observation, students soon pick up that good speakers use repetition more, which guides audiences in following, comprehending, and recalling ideas presented.

Effective speakers tend to use shorter, more declarative sentences comprised of vivid verbs, concrete nouns, graphic images, and even vocabulary chosen for its sound and suggestive power. Carefully selected transitions help hold the speech together while keeping listeners on track with the claim or position, arguments, and stories being presented in informative, persuasive, and entertaining situations.

A thoughtful speaker also takes into consideration what the audience sees as it listens. This begins with attire as well as the use of gestures and physical space. Invite your students to brainstorm places they are likely to speak. They may come up with settings that include your classroom, houses of worship, gyms, auditoriums, banquet halls, or board rooms.

Ask students to give purposeful attention to speakers. Consider offering extra credit for students who attend on-campus or community events where guest speakers are invited to present. See figure 8.1 for a simple-to-assess critique that helps students focus on key rhetorical communication traits. Just offer full credit for a complete on-time critique. The goal is to raise students' consciousness about oral presentations.

Critique of Oral Presentation

Student Name:
Name of speaker:
Location/Place:
Date:
Time of Day:
Occasion:
Title or Topic:
SUMMARY OF PRESENTATION and YOUR RESPONSE
: (Who? What? When? Where? Why? And How?)

Rate 1-5 (low to high), the following characteristics, then summarize in ½ your evaluation of this presentation in sentences with reasons or explanations, and what you especially liked.

Rate 1-5	TRAIT
	CHOICE OF TOPIC: Interesting? Appropriate for audience?
	INTRODUCTION: Creates interest? Previews main ideas?
	BODY: Sufficient information? New or surprising information?
	FORMS OF SUPPORT: Are ideas developed? Are points proven?
	ORGANIZATION: Easy to follow? Moves smoothly from point to point.
	LANGUAGE: Clear? Vivid?
	DELIVERY: Natural? Enthusiastic?
	CONCLUSION: Summarizes main points? Makes central idea memorable.
	EFFECTIVENESS: Carries out speaker's purpose? How did the audience react?

Adapted from form by Wang Tong. Bureau of Educational and Cultural Affairs. OFFICE OF ENGLISH LANGUAGE PROGRAMS (Viewed 8/14/07)
<http://exchanges.state.gov/forum/vols/vol37/no1/p26.htm>

Figure 8.1 Sample critique. *Created by author.*

Figure 8.2 Regularly Plan Random Grouping in person or online. *iStock/Prostock-Studio.*

Speakers also practice their speeches often enough to be able to deliver them at an easy-to-follow speed, using pauses, pacing, and volume to attract and retain attention throughout the speech. Contemporary speakers tend to utilize electronic and digital applications to augment their presentations. The CWPA Outcomes Statement notes that "by the end of the first-year composition, students should . . . Adapt composing processes for a variety of technologies and modalities."[5] But first, these aspiring speakers must consider, other than for the grade, their reason for speaking. Your task now is to challenge students to pattern effective content, structure, and deliveries that fit their audience and purpose, as well as the student's personal style.

DECIDE THE SPECIFIC RHETORICAL PURPOSE

Generally, there are four basic reasons for oral communication: to inform, to persuade, to entertain, and to commemorate. Include assignments for pairs or small groups of students to analyze and critique a variety of sample speeches. Allot time in class to give brief, impromptu speeches. Giving both formal and informal oral presentations provides students with personal experience to reflect on when you give a major assignment with oral and multimodal components. In a virtual setting, have a timer that students can see. If students are studying in an asynchronous class, have students record and upload their impromptu speech earning points for being uploaded by assigned time.

An expository speech could be about something that students already know how to do or something they are learning in a course leading to their major.

A short speech can be a component of their expository writing assignment. A persuasive speech can be a fully researched topic for which students prepare to convince their classmates to give serious consideration or to change their belief or behavior about a current event.

To help students relax giving the speech, you could give them the option to present the speech in the persona of a character from a piece of literature, a person from history, or a notable figure from their field or major. A commemorative speech could be solemn and serious or entertaining and humorous but always in good taste.

VIEW AND CRITIQUE PUBLIC SPEAKERS

An effective in-class assignment is to show videos of public speakers and invite students to critique what they see based on the criteria to be used when the students present their writing as a speech. Check online sources for speeches of 5 to 7 minutes.

Show the entire speech. Have students use the criteria on class rubrics to indicate on a scale of one to five how effective the speech is that they view. Then replay the speech, this time turning off the volume, and have students observe the speaker's use of mannerisms and gestures, use of space, and visual aids. Few lessons reveal more clearly the dual nature of public speaking—it is visual and auditory.

You also could assign for homework that students bring in samples from a link to videos that you provide. Invite students to customize a rubric with criteria to evaluate the kinds of speaking they are viewing. See the companion website for this book: www.planningwithpurpose.info, for sample grading and peer feedback forms to assess speech presentations given in your classes.

PRACTICE BY GIVING A COMMEMORATIVE SPEECH

Here is an in-class activity that introduces features to consider as students prepare to write-for-speaking and give focused attention to their chosen audience and specified purpose. Consider a commemorative speech—giving a toast at a wedding, birthday, awards event, or a reflection at a memorial service. In these instances, the objectives are to keep the speech light, brief, and respectful.

To begin, show a short video like the one on Toastmaster's YouTube channel, "How to Offer a Toast." Next, project a slide with questions like those below. Then, show the video again. Now ask students to write answers to the questions about the speaker's message in the video:

- What advice and/or suggestions given by the speaker in this video can you apply to your next oral presentation? If you disagree with what is presented in the video, what would you suggest to the speaker?
  - Does the speaker's delivery, demeanor, appearance, and so forth, engage you? Why or why not?
  - Explain your reason(s).
- What are three takeaways from this video that can be applied in other settings for oral presentations?

After writing their observations, have the class work in pairs or groups of four to five to discuss their responses for 4–5 minutes. You already know how to create small groups by simply counting class members off by numbers. Another method—have each student's name written on an index card. Shuffle those cards, and, in front of the class, randomly deal them out into four to five piles. This procedure is an efficient way to create manageable small group discussions/activities and works well in classes where most students already know each other. Varying the groups randomly makes it less likely the same students always work together. Doing so also inspires more varied discussions.

Call the class to order and ask a volunteer from each group to share responses to at least one of the questions on the slides. Record student responses on the board or poster. Note where there was consensus and which

Figure 8.3 Have Students Justify Choices for Multimodal Augmentations. *iStock/damircudic.*

questions generated more diverse responses. Encourage students to utilize in their own presentations what works and avoid what doesn't.

Now, the fun begins! Invite one member from each group to give a 1-minute toast to someone special to that speaker: a grandparent, a former coach, a movie star, and so forth. It's okay for students to chuckle, as long as they are courteous. As a follow-up, at another time, use the same video and have the students critique the quality of the video as a multimodal presentation. Adapt the "Rubric for Slideshow and Video," figure 7.2 in chapter 7.

Collaborating, after viewing this video and watching the impromptu presentations gives students the opportunity to express ways to use the delivery strategies for their graded classroom presentations. The simplicity of these videos can lay the groundwork for students' presentations in other classes, or in professional or personal settings. Seeing is believing. As they prepare to speak and to observe their classmates, they see the value of practice.

PICK A TOPIC AND PLAN THE SPEECH

You may design a news-related speech assignment for which students think critically about real-life reasons for persuasive speaking, choose a topic, and begin to conduct their research. Then students write, using the style of citation and documentation required at your college, and give an oral presentation on that current issue.

The issue could be a global problem or one affecting their community. See chapter 5, "Composing Compelling Arguments," for building cases that lead to persuasion. Remind students of the subtle differences: arguments offer opposing views for consideration, while persuasive speeches include a call for action with reasons a change will benefit the audience.

Jessica Hudson, one of our graduate teaching assistant contributors, noted in her reflection that she had students decide on a text-based topic at the beginning of the course. This topic would be one they would investigate for several assignments. She wrote, "This way, I hope they will feel more inclined and less pressured to write about something, 'the professor' thinks they should write about, and instead, choose a topic they truly care about on a more personal level." In other words, no matter the topic, if it is personally meaningful to the students, they are more likely to invest the time to compose effective presentations that are interesting to their audience.

CONSTRUCT THE SPEECH

Your students now recognize that writing to speak is very different from simply writing an essay and reading it aloud. Once students have completed their research and written their first and second drafts, have them adapt that second draft for a speech. Review with them the characteristics of an effective script for speaking.

First, students can focus on revising their draft so that it has shorter, less complex sentences that flow when they speak them. Encourage them to read their speeches aloud and exchange feedback with an in-class partner, practicing their listening and critiquing skills. Vital to your lesson planning is allotting time for students to construct the speech and providing homework guidance for them to practice presenting the speech within given time limits.

Students should check to confirm their manuscript states their goal or position, illustrates with examples, explains it, and reviews that position statement in much the same way they may have learned about P. I. E. patterns in high school. In the P.I.E. structure, writers

- state their POSITION in a claim statement that usually includes an adjective or adverb: "Writing *convincing* arguments takes careful planning."
  "Students who learn to write well will be *better* prepared for careers in any field."
- Use examples. facts, statistics, anecdotes to ILLUSTRATE that POSITION.

Figure 8.4 Remind Students That Oral Presentations Are Both Visual and Auditory.
iStock/Prostock-Studio.

- Pull them together with EXPLANATIONS and reasons that connect and show how those illustrations connect, explain, and substantiate their claim or position statement.

Students practicing these P. I. E. prompts advance steadily toward meeting the CWPA Outcomes goal that says "students should . . . Locate and evaluate (for credibility, sufficiency, accuracy, timeliness, bias and so on) primary and secondary research materials."[6] The rubric for this assignment should be customized to include the kinds of resources required for this written and oral presentation.

As speakers, students are responsible not only for letting their audience know what the speech is about using some kind of verbalized signpost or thesis statement, but also for providing transitions to help the listeners process the information and stay on track. You can further reduce anxiety by sharing questions for students to self-check their speeches to assure they have utilized a variety of explanations and supporting evidence that lead to more successful speeches. See questions in the section on "Self-Checking for Effective Speaking" that follows.

INCORPORATE MULTIMODAL COMPONENTS

Effective presenters rely on various modes of communication to reach a specified audience. Guide your students to incorporate enhancements in their speeches, which aligns your practice with the Conference on College Composition and Communication's Principles of Sound Writing Instruction that states, "Sound writing instruction emphasizes relationships between writing and technologies . . . writers learn about the potential that various technologies have for the production, consumption, and distribution of forms of composed knowledge."[7] Augmenting their presentations using appropriate digital devices helps students communicate with precision and clarity.

Depending on the topic and audience, additions may be props, slides, video, and demonstrations, music or sound effects. (See chapter 7 for features to consider when creating slides as visuals to supplement an oral presentation.) Finally, have students explain in a few written sentences why those additions can clarify their claims and enhance the words the writers plan to speak. Taking time to specify an audience and focus on their prior knowledge and beliefs will help students select and design more effective multimodal presentations.

ORGANIZE ORAL PRESENTATIONS
FOR MAXIMUM IMPACT

An effective speech begins by inviting the audience to listen for a specific purpose and then develop that idea with a variety of evidence that appeals to the head, the heart, and often the pocket. Whether one is speaking to inform, argue or persuade, entertain, or commemorate, the structure of the speech must be considered carefully to be effective.

SELF-CHECK FOR EFFECTIVE SPEAKING

Here are several questions students can ask themselves and their peers as they plan.

1. Does this speech open with an attention-getter that will intrigue the audience to listen?
2. Does the introduction include a *signpost, claim, or thesis statement* that will indicate the order of the arguments to follow?
3. Does this speech clearly show that this topic is important to me (personally, as the literary character or community/historical figure who is being represented)?
4. Does this speech clearly show why this topic is important to my audience?
5. Do I provide adequate support for each main section of my speech? (Write the number of times you include each of these supporting materials in your speech.

   Have students check types of evidence they use

_____Illustrations/examples	_____Explanations
_____Definitions	_____Restatements
_____Statistics/numbers	_____Humor
_____Comparison/contrast	_____Opinion of experts
_____Testimony	_____Quotations

6. Does the speech include signal words (transitions) that show the relationship between and among ideas?
7. Does the speech close with a call for action? Does the call flow smoothly from the arguments presented in the body of the speech?

Having students write a script of their speech is also a practical way to have them practice sentence syntax and flow. Their goal is to communicate clearly in both writing and speaking, using Standard English, or otherwise. Their choice of grammar and vocabulary or jargon appropriate for their specific audience makes the difference in how well they get their ideas across and achieve their goal of bringing about change in their audience's beliefs or behaviors.

PERSONALIZE MULTIMODAL PRESENTATIONS

A short assignment offering students choice and personalization as they practice rhetorical composition skills to inform, argue, persuade, commemorate, or entertain can be based on art. Invite students to

- identify a single work of art they love and admire,
- compose a 250–300 word written description, then,
- give a 2–3-minute oral presentation with multimodal components.

Students may choose to write about a film, a story, a piece of music, a painting, a sculpture or even a car—anything to them that represents art. Most presentations are likely to (1) inform, by describing the art, (2) argue with reasons the art is worthy of admiration, and (3) entertain or commemorate with images, props, video, or music that may persuade their classmates to change their thinking about the student's choice of art.

PRACTICE, PRACTICE, PRACTICE

Insist that your students arrange with at least three different listeners to get feedback on their presentations before giving them in class for evaluation. This listener could be a friend, family member, or a classmate. Practicing aloud is the only way for students to know for certain they know the content of their presentation well enough to deliver it with confidence, (1) making eye contact, (2) using gestures, (3) pronouncing words correctly and clearly, (4) varying the pace of speaking, and (5) maintaining their poise within the time allotted for the speech.

Students sometimes wonder what they should be paying attention to when they practice a speech. Strongly suggest that they time themselves as they give their speech at least three times, standing in front of a mirror, holding their notes on the index cards, cell phone, or tablet they plan to use when they give their speech in public. If they are using props or showing slides, they must practice with them. Have printed notes for backup.

If the students can look up at themselves in the mirror and keep talking throughout their speech, they probably are prepared to look up and make more frequent eye contact with their audience. Their notes should have

DAY	RED	GREEN	PURPLE	ORANGE	BLUE
1	SPEAKING (NO FEEDBACK)	Comment on *CONTENT* (Appropriate for audience, variety of support, appeals, quality of evidence and resources, sources cited, etc.)	Comment on *ORGANIZATION* (Introduction with SIGN POST (statement of purpose) TRANSITIONS (appropriate for kind of speech) CONCLUSION (summary, reflection, or projection without introducing new ideas)	Comment on *VOCAL ISSUES* (Articulation, intonation, pace, pauses, volume, etc.)	Comment on *APPEARANCE* (Appropriate gestures, use of physical space, visual aids, etc.)
2	APPEARANCE	SPEAKING	CONTENT	ORGANIZATION	VOCAL ISSUES
3	VOCAL ISSUES	APPEARANCE	SPEAKING	CONTENT	ORGANIZATION
4	ORGANIZATION	VOCAL ISSUES	APPEARANCE	SPEAKING	CONTENT
5	CONTENT	ORGANIZATION	VOCAL ISSUES	APPEARANCE	SPEAKING

Figure 8.5   Include Visual, Aural and Vocal Criteria on Feedback Forms. *Created by author.*

keywords and a few full sentences; otherwise, the student speaker will be tempted to read rather than talk to the audience.

Encourage students to wear something special on the day they give or video record the speech, an outfit that is especially neat, comfortable, and appropriate for their intended audience and setting. Choosing what to wear reminds them that people in an audience are spectators, influenced by the speaker's physical appearance and posture. Recommend that your students make an audio or video recording and listen and watch to hear and see what others are to hear and see when they deliver their oral presentations.

EVALUATE ARGUMENTATIVE AND PERSUASIVE SPEECHES

Since public speaking is both an oral and visual way of communicating, the criteria used to assess student presentations should take into consideration both elements. Share with your students the criteria you will use to measure their progress. Providing students with probing questions helps them evaluate their speech plans and encourages students to modify their speeches before presenting them to the public. For example, if you assign a speech to persuade, ask students to include arguments with a range of appeals.

- Does this speech make appeals to the head (definitions, statistics, explanations, and comparison/contrast)?
- Does this speech make appeals to the heart (humor, explanation, illustrations, quotations, testimony or stories about real people)?
- Does this speech make appeals to the pocket (definitions, facts, statistics, and comparison/contrast related to money)?
- Does this speech include verbal evidence to show sources of borrowed evidence, or quotations? "According to . . . ."
- Does the speaker speak clearly, varying the pace to allow time for the audience to absorb ideas?
- Does the speaker use gestures and visual aids that reinforce and expand audience understanding rather than distract?

To prepare for a week of speeches, have students sign up in rainbow color groups that will present their speeches on a specified day. Each color group is assigned to comment on one aspect of speech delivery each day, except the day members are scheduled to give their speech. Note that on one day, one panel of students in the audience comments on content, another day on organization, another day on the use of visuals, and on another day vocal qualities of the presenter. While students in the audience focus on one trait a day, the speakers receive comments about all four traits on the grading rubric. If working asynchronously, set a date and time when students must post the responses to viewing the video speeches of their classmates.

CONCLUSION

When students spend time observing, analyzing, and pointing out the qualities of a good speech presentation, they become attuned to differences in the effectiveness. Then, when given time to research, write, and practice, they no longer are content simply to give a report but endeavor to give an oral presentation that has meaning for them and engages their audience. Students become eager and able to develop the writing and speaking skills that help them communicate more successfully in any rhetorical situation, for personal or professional reasons.

NOTES

1. Clella Jaffe, "Introduction to Public Speaking and Culture," in *Public Speaking: Concepts and Skills for a Diverse Society*, 5th ed. (Belmont, CA: Wadsworth/Thomas Learning, 2007), 6.

2. Kettering College Writing Center, "Multimodal Projects," accessed March 29, 2020, https://kcwritingcenter. weebly.com/multimodal-projects.html.

3. Council of Writing Program Administrators, "WPA Outcomes Statement for First-Year Composition (3.0)."

4. Ibid.

5. Ibid.

6. Ibid.

7. Conference of College Composition and Communication, "Principles of the Teaching of Postsecondary Writing Position Statement." Last modified March 2015. https://cccc.ncte.org/cccc/resources/positions/postsecondarywriting (accessed April 21, 2020).

Afterword

Education is the passport to the future, for tomorrow belongs to those who prepare for it today.[1]

—Malcolm X

You are now a teacher with honor and responsibility, entrusted with the lives and learning of the students assigned to you. At first, the ups and downs on the road may seem an endless trek up a curvaceous mountain trail. But, as you focus on growth, not grades, progress, not speed, you can safely traverse the rolling hills and triumphantly reach the journey's end.

Just steer steadily forward, accelerating and slowing down as needs arise. Yes, you may creep and climb up some of those steeper hills and sometimes may need to slow down and bumble across potholes created by inclement weather, technical issues, or natural disasters beyond your control. Rest assured; others have traveled the roads before you. You can make it, too.

On the way, maximize opportunities to consult with veteran educators in your department. You just may have an experience similar to what Shanika Carter had the first year she taught in community college. This contributor acknowledged, "my department head was someone who served as a mentor and helping me to acclimate well to the campus and the department curriculum." If you seek them, you, too, may find willing mentors to help you make it safely, thus maintaining your morale along the way.

Share the driving, listen to back seat drivers, but resist relinquishing control. Pay attention to road signs pointing to the progress you are making together. Do remember to stop regularly to refuel, maximize incidental side trips that can enrich the spirit and inspire the soul, but quickly return to the main path, keeping your eyes on the goal.

Figure A.1 Plan Carefully and Enjoy the Journey. *iStock/qunamax.*

As you design lessons that respect the knowledge and experience each student brings and challenges each one to build on them both, success is assured for you all. Remember, too, that what you have read here are descriptions, not prescriptions. You can adapt, adjust, and adopt to fit your current situation and department content resources. You may choose to do something very different for each teaching setting!

With a firm hand on the wheel, visualizing a mental map of the course, you can safely negotiate this first time or first year and reach your shared destination, each of you wiser and more confident writers and educators than when the expedition first began.

NOTE

1. Malcolm X, Brainy Quotes, accessed March 10, 2020.

Bibliography

Bacon, Francis. 2015. "Thoughts On The Business Life." Accessed April 2, 2020. https://www.forbes.com/quotes/2933/.

Conference on College Composition & Communication. 2015. "Principles for the Postsecondary Teaching of Writing." March. Accessed April 21, 2020. https://cccc.ncte.org/cccc/resources/positions/postsecondarywriting.

Conference on College Composition & Communication. 2016. "Statement on Language, Power, and Action." Accessed April 21, 2020. https://cccc.ncte.org/cccc/language-power-action.

Conference of College Composition and Communication. 2014. "Writing Assessment Position Statement." Last Modified November 2014. Accessed April 20, 2020. https://cccc.ncte.org/cccc/resources/positions/writingassessment.

Council of Writing Program Administrators. 2019. "WPA Outcomes Statement for First-Year Composition (3.0)." July 18. Accessed March 19, 2020. http://wpacouncil.org/aws/CWPA/pt/sd/news_article/243055/_PARENT/layout_details/false.

Ellison, Ralph. 1998. "Hidden Name and Complex Fate." In *Shadow and Act*, by Ralph Ellison, 148. New York, Y: Random House, Inc.

España, Carla and Luz Yadira Herrera. "Lessons for Centering the Voices and Experiences of Bilingual Latinx Students." *California English*, Volume 25, No. 4 (May 2020), p. 33.

Franklin, Benjamin. 2020. *Quotes.net*. Accessed April 2, 2020. https://www.quotes.net/quote/3919.

Hammerstein, Oscar. 2020. "Getting to Know You Lyrics." Accessed March 6, 2020. https://www.stlyrics.com/lyrics/thekingandi/gettingtoknowyou.htm.

Hansen, Heather. 2020. "Speak English Clearly and Grammatically and Boost Your Success!" Accessed April 3, 2020. https://www.streetdirectory.com/travel_guide/191314/phones/speak_english_clearly_and_grammatically_and_boost_your_success.html.

Jaffe, Clella. 2007. "Introduction to Public Speaking and Culture." In *Public Speaking: Concepts and Skills for a Diverse Society*, by Clella Jaffe. Belmont, CA: Thomas Learning, p. 6.

Kettering College Writing Center. 2020. "Kettering College Writing Center Multimodal Projects." Accessed March 29, 2020. https://kcwritingcenter.weebly.com/multimodal-projects.html.

Mackenzie, Jock. 2007. *Essay Writing: Teaching the Basics from the Ground Up*. Pembroke, NH: Pembroke Publishers.

Moberg, Goran "George". 1984. *Writing in Groups: New Techniques for Good Writing without Drills*, 3rd ed. New York: The Writing Consultant.

Nelson, Russell M. 2020. "Accomplishing the Impossible Quotes." Accessed March 19, 2020. https://www.goodreads.com/work/quotes/47216368-accomplishing-the-impossible-what-god-does-what-we-can-do.

Pascal, Blaise. 2020. "Blaise Pascal Quotes." Accessed April 2, 2020. https://www.brainyquote.com/quotes/blaise_pascal_133403.

Roseboro, Anna J. Small. 1989. "Writing and Learning Groups in Math." University of California, San Diego.

Schrock, Kathy. 2020. "Kathy Schrock's Guide to Everything." April 6. Accessed April 2020. https://www.schrockguide.net/assessment-and-rubrics.html.

Schulten, Katherine. 2001. "The New York Times Learning Network: Teaching & Learning with The New York Times." January 19. Accessed April 2020. https://learning.blogs.nytimes.com/2001/01/19/state-of-the-art/.

Ward, William Arthur. 2020. "William Arthur Ward Quotes." Accessed March 6, 2020. https://www.brainyquote.com/authors/william-arthur-ward-quotes.

X, Malcolm. 2020. "Malcolm X Quotes." Accessed March 10, 2020. https://www.brainyquote.com/quotes/malcolm_x_386475.

Zinsser, William. 2020. "Writing to Learn Quotes." Accessed March 6, 2020. https://www.goodreads.com/work/quotes/572323-writing-to-learn#:~:text=.

Index

admit slip, 45
appropriate: assessment, 90; comments, 48, 86, 96; grammar, 35
art: inspire writing, 70; of rhetoric, 82; to teach essay structure, 70
assessment(s): collaborative, 45; formative, 13–14, 48, 50, 55, 76, 91; informal, 16, 21, 48, 69; no-stress, 50; share standards, 9, 86; summative, 90. *See also* Chapter 1: "Preparing to be Efficient and Effective", 1–18
audience, 36, 52, 60–61, 66, 78, 79, 89, 99

behavior: classroom guidelines, 2, 7, 9; observation notes, 58, 76, 77, 98

challenges: to grading, 10–11; to students, xiii, 16, 30; to teacher, 16, 20, 27
choice, choose: language, 102; student, 8, 10, 12, 55, 78, 109, 111
class management. *See* grouping (group(s); organization; timers; Chapter 1: "Preparing to be Efficient and Effective", 1–18
code switching, blending, 34–35

collaboration: among students, 8, 16, 43, 74, 96, 104; among teachers, 4
community: audience, 12; ethnicity, 36; project, 36, 101; vulnerability in learning community, 18, 21, 27
Conference of Writing Program Administrators, 31, 51, 60, 74, 79, 83, 102
Conference on College Composition and Communication, 33, 107
conferencing, conference(s), with students, 50, 74–75
critical thinking, 41
culture(s) relevance: community, 20, 89; ethnicity. *See* ethnicities; language, 35; religions, 39; respect, 2, 39; students, 93
curriculum, curricula: college, 52; flexibility, 52; goals, 3, 15, 22, 50; other content areas, 74, 89
customize rubrics, 10, 73, 96, 105
CWPA. *See* Conference of Writing Program Administrators

dialect(s), vernacular: academic, 34; blending. *See* code-switching; English Language Learners, 93; honoring, 24, 35, 39; regional, 34, 35, 38, 39; vernacular, 34 digital devices: cell phones, 39, 54, 109; games, 16, 92; general use, 6, 27; laptops, notebooks, tablets, 17; prepping students for use, 6–7; projector, 15–16, 59, 67, 71; timer, 7, 14, 17, 28–29, 53–54, 57, 71, 73, 102; viewing media, 7, 82, 107. *See also* Chapter 1: "Preparing to be Efficient and Effective", 1–18

edit, editing: in groups, 19; peer editing, 27, 62, 73–74, 96; self-edit writing, 8, 13, 108
essay: analyzing, 16, 33, 44, 79, 82; argumentative. *See* Chapter 6: "Composing Compelling Arguments", 63–78; citations, 48, 68, 91; compare/contrast, 67; different from speech, 105; five-paragraph, 53; graphics, 56, 67, 70, 100; informative. *See* Chapter 5: "Engaging Expository Writing", 51–62; narrative, 14, 19, 25; personal, 23, 51, 89, 101; persuasive. *See* Chapter 7: "Writing Persuasively to Impact Thinking and Behavior", 79–98; physically act out, 60; response to art, 71, 86; structure, 67, 73, 85; train as metaphor, 70
ethnicities, 2, 4, 37
exit slip, 47
expository/informative writing: assignments, 51–52, 61, 67, 102; feedback ideas, 57, 62; rubrics, 55. *See also* Chapter 5: "Engaging Expository Writing", 51–62
extra credit, 9, 12, 60, 77, 101

games, 16, 52, 92
genre, 33, 86, 99
grading: efficient, 12; grammar, 48, 109; guidelines, xiv, 75; load, 12, 14; rubrics. *See* rubrics; self-reflections, 13, 49; ungraded, 13, 28, 41–42, 50, 76, 91, 101; weighting, 13
grammar: cultural sensitivity, xiv, 30, 33, 56, 71, 92; grading for, 28; honoring student's, 35, 39; nonstandard, 40, rules, 33, 40; in speech, public speaking, 34, 39, 99, 109; Standard English, 35; syntax, 35, 108; traditional. *See* Chapter 3: "Understanding Grammars to Negotiate Conventions", 33–40. *See also* Chapter 8: "Writing for Speaking and Multimodal Presentations", 99–112
graphic organizer, 67, 70
groups, grouping students: collaborating; 68, 104; (for presentations, 36; for recitation, 68–69, 104; for writing, 24, 47); discussion, 14, 16, 35, 83; general, xv, 45, 53, 58; virtual, 7. *See also* Chapter 2: "Networking with Narratives to Cultivate Community", 19–31

homework: assigning, xiv, 6, 8, 14, 16, 59, 73, 96, 103; grading, 8, 26; purpose(s), 8, 44

inclusion, 19
informative/expository writing. *See* Chapter 5: "Engaging Expository Writing, 51–62.

kinesthetic learning, 16, 53–54

listening: to speeches, 96, 108, 110; by students, 14, 25, 38, 65, 93, 100, 110; by teacher, 47, 53, 113

media: arts. *See* Chapter 8: "Writing for Public Speaking and Media", 99–112; resources, 16, 38, 82, 86, 97, 100; specialist, 4; technology use. *See* technology

multimodal: assignments, 36, 78, 99, 109; for teaching, 53, 56, 72

narrative writing: assignments, 14, 19, 25; human interest, 29. *See also* Chapter 2: "Networking with Narratives to Cultivate Community", 19–31; names, 25; writing program administration outcome goals, 19
National Writing Project, xv, 14

organization, organize: for class management, 54; classroom resources, 6, 15; for essay, 87; graphically, 67; grouping students. *See* groups, grouping; for oral presentations, 95, 107; research information, 59. *See also* Chapter 1: "Preparing to be Effective and Efficient"

patterning, patterns: author's style, 22, 59, 67; grammar, 32; P.I.E. paragraph, 106; speech, 101; train as metaphor, 70
pedagogy, xv, 37, 55
peer feedback/response. *See* Chapter 1: "Plan Now to be Efficient and Effective", 1–18
personal connections, experiences: in essays, 29, 51; honor privacy, 21; in speeches, 101, 105; with students, 72
personalize: classroom, 4; instruction, 6; office, 4; presentations, 6; website, 6
personal stories: author's, 25, 34; students', 2, 25, 89, 93; teachers', 25, 93
persuade, persuasion, persuasive: advertisements, 82, 94; speaking, 107. *See also* Chapter 3: "Networking with Narratives to Cultivate Community", 33–40; Writing. *See* Chapter 7: "Writing Persuasively to Impact Thinking and Behavior", 79–98

Planning with Purpose website connections, companion website, 31, 43, 53, 70, 103
policies: attendance, 9, 17; extra credit, 12; late work, 9, 12
practice: citation of sources, 87, 90, 95, 110; collaboration/cooperation, 8, 18, 42, 74, 103; evaluating websites, 73, 79; grammar rules, 34, 39; guided, 72, 90; listening, 16, 61, 65, 100, 108; metacognition, 8, 42; for speeches, 52, 60, 101, 104, 107; using research resources, 19, 22, 54, 65, 84, 90, 105; working collaboratively, 8, 18, 42, 74, 104; for writing, 14
presentations, student: oral, 33, 53, 67, 77, 91, 100, 104, 110; visual, 83, 99, 106, 109
processes: grouping students, 7, 16, 27, 73, 110; homework rationale, options, 8; in-class activities, 6, 14, 16, 45, 71, 92, 103; movement for learning, 16, 55; on-line commenting, 28, 73, 96; reading(s), approaches, sources, 25; using classroom space, 54; writing process (National Writing Project), xv. *See also* Chapter 1: "Preparing to be Efficient and Effective", 1–18
public speaking: writing for speaking, 106; *See* Chapter 8: "Writing for Speaking and Multimodal Presentations", 99–112

R.A.G., Read around group, 27
revision strategies: Five E's, explain, expand, exchange, expunge, enliven, 85
rhetorical knowledge: Definition, 1, 36; Writing Program Administration Outcome Goals, 1. *See also* Chapter 6 "Composing Compelling Arguments", 63–78

rubrics: with assignments, 83; prepping for conference, 75; self-check, 106; Six Traits©, 9; for student feedback, 9, 11

scaffolding, 7, 13, 85
social justice, inclusion, 35
S.P.A.R., Spontaneous Argumentation, 65
student choice: on assignments, 55, 72; dialect, 34; grades, 10; Standard English, 39, 109
student(s): critical thinkers, 79; getting to know. See Chapter 2: "Networking with Narratives to Cultivate Community", 19–31

technology. See "digital devices"
TED Talks, 82, 100
think, pair, share, 15
timers: for group work, 28; to manage class time, 7, 14, 17, 57, 102; for quick-writes, 25
translanguaging, 37

trigger issues: ethnicity, 2, 35, 38; politics, 80, 93; race, 35; religion, 2, 39, 84, 89

virtual learning, xiii, 5, 7, 15–17, 46–47, 54, 73, 75, 102
vocabulary: academic, 26, 82; audience, 108; choosing, 51, 100; content area, 45; jargon, 10, 109

writing in content areas. See Chapter 4: "Writing to Clarify Thinking", 41–50
Writing Programs Administration Outcome Goals: analysis, 32, 49, 56; argument, 60, 100; general goals, 17, 22, 56, 74, 79, 86; literacy in content areas, 34, 97; media literacy, 6; narrative, 19; persuasive, 79; public speaking. See Chapter 8: " Writing for Speaking and Multimodal Presentations", 99–112; research, 23, 90; speaking, 99

About the Contributors*

José Luis Cano—BA, MA; PhD student in Rhetoric and Composition, Texas Christian University; former adjunct instructor of adult students at Texas Southernmost College, a predominantly Latina/o community college in Brownsville, Texas.

Shanika Carter—BA, MS; instructor at Montcalm Community College in Sidney, Michigan, and Muskegon Community College in Muskegon, Michigan.

Kelsie Endicott—BFA, MFA; EdD in progress, Salisbury University, Salisbury, Maryland; taught at Community College of Baltimore County, Maryland; writing tutor at Salisbury University.

Jessica Hudson—BA; MFA. in Creative Writing in progress, Northern Michigan University, Marquette, Michigan; graduate teaching assistant at Northern Michigan University.

Mallory Jones—BA; MA in English in progress, Northern Michigan University, Marquette, Michigan; graduate teaching assistant at Northern Michigan University.

Roz Roseboro—BA; MBA; MFA in Creative Writing in progress, Northern Michigan University, Marquette, Michigan; graduate teaching assistant at Northern Michigan University.

Tiffany Stachnik—BA; MA in English in progress; graduate teaching assistant at Northern Michigan University in Marquette, Michigan.

*See our companion website for full text of contributors' reflections: www.planningwithpurpose.info.

About the Authors

Anna J. Small Roseboro, wife, mother, and National Board Certified Teacher, has over four decades of experience teaching in public, parochial, and private schools, mentoring early career educators, and facilitating leadership institutes. She has taught students in five different states across the country, served as director of summer school programs, and chaired her English department. Anna has published six textbooks based on these experiences. The California Association of Teachers of English and the National Council of Teachers of English each awarded her their Distinguished Service Awards.

Claudia A. Marschall taught English and Theater Arts for the Buffalo Public Schools (B.P.S) in Buffalo, New York. Through the B.P.S. Mentor Teacher Internship Program, she supported early career and newly hired English Language Arts (ELA) teachers. Claudia cochaired a sub-committee of the National Council of Teachers of English (NCTE). She cohosted the session "Nuts and Bolts for New ELA Teachers" at several NCTE annual conventions.

Claudia enjoys working behind the scenes with local theater groups, attending concerts with her husband, traveling, and spending time with family and friends.

www.ingramcontent.com/pod-product-compliance
Lightning Source LLC
Chambersburg PA
CBHW030143240426
43672CB00005B/240